THE LIFE AND DEATH OF
DR MARTIN LUTHER

The passages whereof have been taken out of his own and other godly and most learned men's writings, who lived in his time.

1 Thessalonians 5:12-13: We beseech you, brethren, to know them. Who labor among you, etc., and to esteem them very highly for their work sake, and be at peace among yourselves:

LONDON Printed by I. L. for John Stafford, and are to be sold at his shop in Chancery Lane, over against the Rolls: 1643.

Berith Press
P.O. Box 861, Kansas, OK 74347
(918) 896-2055
www.berithpress.com

The Life and Death of Dr Martin Luther was first published in 1641. In this Berith Press reprint, in which spelling, grammar, and formatting changes have been made. With thanks to EEBO-TCP for the corpus of texts it has produced. Printed in the U.S.A.

ISBN 978-1-963516-20-3

TO
THE RIGHT HONORABLE
SIR THOMAS ROE

Knight, Chancellor of the Most Noble
Order of the Garter, and one of His Majesty's
Most Honorable Privy
Council:

O whom rather should I address this present discourse, than to your honorable self, who – by your extraordinary embassy for His Majesty of England into Germany – well observed the country and the present estate thereof, where many passages here mentioned were acted. And much the rather do I humbly present it to your honorable patronage, because, upon that happy occasion, it pleased our gracious God to put then into your mind and to nourish therein ever since, a serious consideration of the deplorable distractions of the Christian church; as he did into good

II

Nehemiah's mind, of the lamentable estate of Jerusalem in his time.[1]

Your compassionate and tender affection was, and is still much moved to observe the living stones of the New Jerusalem lying in the dust,[2] or drenched in their own blood, some of her priests and their flocks clad in sackcloth, others with their people by sword and fire cast out and banished; and which is worst of all, your honor well discerned how difficult a task it was to cure this fearful malady: because disaffection of parties and dissention of opinions – unless God prevented the mischief – would not admit the binding up of the wound.

Nor did these miserable calamities of God's people only vex and grieve your pious and religious soul, but also so roused and summoned up Your Honor's most serious thoughts, that with a hearty and godly providence,[3] with a sincere and prudent circumspection you presently consulted with other most learned, religious and Christian lovers of God's church about the peace thereof, so far as possibly may be attained, and so far as it lies in the power of Christian princes, of most judicious divines, and of truly zealous people, guided by them both: that as much as may

---

[1] Nehemiah 1 & 2

[2] Segnius irritant animos demissa per aures, quam quae sunt oculis subjecta sidelibus, Hor.

[3] As the good Samaritan not only pitied, but took care of the wounded man.

be, we may all be of one mind and accord, and think, and speak one and the same thing, as the sacred Scripture often and straightly gives us in charge.[4]

For this end, Mr. John Dury – a divine of singular piety and learning, truly studious of the church's peace, and incomparably sedulous to advance the same, and first interested in the work by your honorable means and encouragement – has so much prevailed with many illustrious princes and states,[5] and the most eminent learned men in Germany, and the parts adjoining, that the work is very well promoted, and a hearty inclination wrought towards a good correspondence for ecclesiastical peace. God grant your honor life and health, that to your great comfort, and all true Christians' joy, you may shortly see the work come to more maturity and perfection.

Amidst Your Honor's grave and weighty intentions for this and other occasions of much concernment, may you please to reflect on this discourse. I conceive that there are many passages therein very considerable for these and after times: and that they will make much for the exciting of our thankfulness to God. When we behold from what beginnings, in [just over 100] years, God's truth has risen, and papistical and Anabaptistical error [has] fallen. It is

---

[4] Christians should be peaceable one with another: the devil and the world raise stirs to many to molest the church.

[5] This by several instruments signed by them will plainly appear.

IV

remarkable that the points by Dr. Luther mainly opposed were indulgences, the pope's boundless power, merit of works, purgatory, communion but in one kind: all chief points and palpably and undeniably gross.[6] And on the other side, that he stood up against the Anabaptists' rebaptization of themselves, their not baptizing infants (as not commanded by Christ) their having all things in common (as had the primitive Christians, Acts 2:44) and against the Antinomians heresies concerning the law, and other like erroneous fancies.

It is also observable that Dr. Luther – striking at the pope's unlawful power – never sought to exalt himself to honor or riches. For though, as he says, he himself with other learned men executed episcopal authority in visiting the churches of Saxony, and reforming things amiss; yet he – knowing his talent fittest for the chair of Wittenberg – never would rise higher; but wrote a book concerning Christian episcopacy, and installed Nicolaus von Amsdorf, Bishop of Neoburg, and George Anhaltinus Bishop of Mersburg.

And in regard that Luther studied and read as professor, philosophy of diverse kinds, was well versed in the [church] fathers, and in Aquinas, Scotus, Occam, and other Schoolmen, and attained to the Greek and Hebrew

---

[6] When walled cities and castles are taken, villages must yield. Isor.

tongues: he was thereby enabled rightly and soundly and gravely,⁷ and not ignorantly, rashly, or humorously to judge of these studies, and of their use in theology.⁸

It was also very commendable in him that he disliked railing discourse without solid and concluding arguments, slighted foolish and groundless calumnies, reproved young students forward and rash attempts without authority for the promoting of his cause, blamed the heady and disorderly tumults raised by the boors and vulgar sort, confessed ingenuously his doubting of some points, his ignorance in others, and craved pardon, if having been lately a popish monk, he should in any point err from the truth.

Seeing as this was Dr. Luther's prudent and religious course, I shall never marvel at his heroic spirit,⁹ and impregnable confidence of God's assistance, and of the success of his attempts; and on very good ground famous and worthy princes countenanced and assisted him, as a man, by his then opposites, convicted of no error, doing much good service in the university, offering his cause to any just trial, appealing from the pope to the general

---

⁷ He left his wife and three children in want and distress to manifest a sign thereof.
⁸ Some who know nothing dote about questions and strife of words, etc. 1 Timothy 6:4.
⁹ The cause required it. And God sweetly moderated Luther's vehemence with P. Melanchthon's mild and calm temper.

council, and in his whole course manifesting a true correspondence of his life with his doctrine.[10]

Much more I might here add, but will not longer detain your honor from the discourse itself. I humbly beseech our gracious God, who enabled Dr. Luther to be an excellent instrument for the reformation of the Christian church, for beating down of error, and setting up of God's truth, that he would implant in us all, quiet, temperate, and Christian affections, and love of Christ's name,[11] and still more and more perfect the settling of truth, and building up of his church, until we all become living stones in the spiritual temple fitted for our God.

The same God of peace crown your honorable self, and all sincere promoters of Christian peace, with peace external and internal here, and with eternal bliss hereafter. So prays he, who is,

Your Honor's ever to be commanded,

Thomas Hayne.

---

[10] Lutheri vitam apud nos, nemo non probat. Eras Epist. lib. 5.

[11] Luthor endured not to have anyone called a *Lutheran*. And Erasmus says, Prorsus odi ista dissidiorum nomina: Christi sumus omnes. lib. Ep. 2.

Christian Reader

AVID – a man after God's own heart, as in other respects so especially in not forgetting any of God's benefits, but frequently and sweetly descanting on them in his sacred songs of praise, among many other blessings – mentions God's gracious leading his people out of Egypt, and teaching them by the ministry of Moses and Aaron. The like thankfulness to God should we show in our hymns of glory to God,[12] as for infinite other favors in these later times, so especially for our coming out of the spiritual Egypt, by the ministry of Dr. Martin Luther.

The goodness of God to the Israelites and us is much alike in both these our deliverances. For when Egypt's tyranny was grown to extremity, and Rome's heresies at full maturity, God seasonably put to his hand, and by Moses then bred up in Pharaoh's court, and by Dr. Luther lately trained up in monkery, showed alike mercy to us both. However men did project to bend the excellent

---

[12] These are a chief and excellent work of the New Testament church. Rev. 4. Rev. 7. 11, 12. Rev. 15. 3.

endowments of these worthy men to their own purposes, God turned them to better use, and seasoning them with his grace, fitted them for the confusion of the Old and New Egypts.

God will be plainly known to have matters of great importance at his own disposing.[13] He of his great goodness directs to the right object his servants' ardent zeal to do good: as in judgment he lets the malicious and envious zeal of both Egypts persist in an evil course to their overthrow. Hence it was, that as God took off St. Paul from his blind and unseasonable zeal for Moses' law in the Pharisaical way, and bent it to the advancing of the gospel; so he quelled Luther's raging fury and intent to vex and kill the opposers of the pope,[14] and put a zealous spirit in him for the maintenance of sacred truth, and the downfall of popish superstition.

And indeed rightly did Erasmus judge that those corrupt times called for a sharp and lancing and searing surgeon to cure their long festered maladies.[15] For the worship of God and the truth of religion was then (as amongst the Israelites in Elijah's time) much depraved and defaced, and required a magnanimous and undaunted spirit, like to that in Elijah, to reform matters extremely out of

---

[13] When the event is seen, then we can observe how God's hand was in the work.

[14] As St. Paul did to vex and kill Christians, Acts 9:1 & 22:19

[15] Epist. B. 14. pag. 453.

frame. Erasmus saw full well how difficult a task Dr. Luther underwent, and for his own part and undertaking was assured that if the knowledge of good arts,[16] of polite learning, of the original tongues, of the sacred Scripture flourished, that the dark fogs of popery could not long continue undispelled. And therefore he complied with all princes,[17] and men studious of good letters whatsoever,[18] to make a knowing world: and would in no wise, though earnestly set upon both by loving entreaties and kind usage, as also by bitter calumnies, and harsh railings of the Pontificians, do any thing of special moment [*weightiness*] against Luther. He was confident that if Luther – being violently opposed and maliced – should fail, yet the truth of Christ, by the light of all good literature and God's blessing, would, maugre [*despite*] all the papists' malice, get the upper hand, and spread itself.

But God was abundantly gracious to Dr. Luther, and made him, as Jeremiah,[19] a defended city, an iron pillar, and a wall of brass, against which his antagonists could in no wise prevail. Had a spirit of pride or contention, or any by-respect set Luther on work against the pope, or had he

---

[16] He foresaw that by these *Novum saeculum brevi exoriturum.* lib. Epist. 3.
[17] Even with George Duke of Sax. whom Luther found most opposite to the Gospel. Eras. epist. B. 12 pag. 430.
[18] He praised some for learning, that they might strive to be praiseworthy for it. Epist. pag. 351.
[19] Jeremiah 1:18

stood upon litigious questions, or [those] of an indifferent nature, he could never have begun with that courage, gone forward with that confidence, [or] come off with that honor, which he did. The blessing of God and a good conscience bore him out, to take such incredible pains in reading, preaching, translating, commenting, disputing, writing, advising the political state, directing the ecclesiastical, restraining the papists fury from open war, counseling some Protestants from too hasty proceedings, preventing tumultuous designs, avoiding secret traps set for him, and in daily praying to God for the prosperity of the gospel.

All true Christians will heartily bless God for him, and his resolute and happy beginning of Reformation. If Papists who notoriously defamed and slandered him in his lifetime, persist still to calumniate him after his death,[20] God in the last day will be judge between them. Luther was (and who is not?) subject to such weaknesses as humanity makes incident to the best men. He knew his slips, he acknowledged them, [and] he craved pardon for them. Yea, he considering that he was a man, and might err, entrusted

---

[20] Men may judge something now by the good effect of his labors.

his learned and faithful friend Melanchthon to revise and moderate some of his tenets after his decease.[21]

In brief, Luther's faith was admirably strong in his God, his labors and studies of singular benefit to God's church, his books and writings very many and learned, his life most pious, and therefore his death full of comfort and blessed.

Accept (good reader) this treatise now presented unto you in an English dress, out of the learned and laborious work of Melchior Adamus; and expect the lives of other most godly and reverend fathers in God's church, and worthy champions, against the enemies of God's truth, both English and foreign: some whereof were never extant before, others, but sparingly in English set forth; all of them worthy of everlasting memory for their promoting of God's glory, and their love to Christian truth. These will shortly appear from the pens of sundry reverend, religious, and faithful divines amongst us.

[May] God make all these labors useful to God's people, and us all thankful for his divine and gracious goodness to these last and worst times.

Yours in all Christian offices,

Thomas Hayne

---

[21] These two by conjoining their studies settled truth: whereas in the Council of Trent, though some divines saw the truth, yet the major part confirmed error.

To the precious memory of *Dr. Martin Luther*.

ELL fare those gentle quills (whose ere they be)
Whose meritorious labors shall set free
The urn imprisoned dust of that renowned
Thrice famous Luther: let his head be crowned
With sacred immortality, and raised
Much rather to be wondered at than praised.
Let babes unborn, like fruitful plants bring forth
To after days new monuments of his worth,
And time-outlasting name: that Babel's whore
And all her bald-pate panders may even roar
For very anguish, and then gnaw and bite
Their tongues for malice, and their nails for spite,
Whilst men made perfect in his well-known story
May all turn patrons, and protect his glory.

Francis Quarles.

HEN blackest clouds of Romish errors base,
Had quite o'erspread truth's amiable face,
And Antichrist's o'ertopping tyranny
Had chained all Europe to idolatry;
Then, suddenly and strangely God did raise
(To Rome's deep admiration and amaze)
Renowned Martin Luther, dauntlessly
To vindicate his truth, and Rome defy.
He, maugre all their spight and fury fell,
Did papal fogs of error clean expel;
Clearing the sun of truth to such pure light
As, ever since, has shone abroad most bright.
Of Hercules his club, what talk we, then?
Since Rome is ruined with great Luther's pen.

I. Vicars.

THE
LIFE AND DEATH
of Dr. *Martin Luther*

HE family of the Luthers was ancient, and spread into diverse parts of the territories of the Earl of Mansfield. It consisted of the middle degree of men. The parents of Martin Luther first lived in Isleben, a town in that earldom; thence they went to dwell in Mansfield, the place of which the earldom took its name.[22] There John Luther, father of Martin, possessed metal mines, bore office, and for his integrity was in good esteem among the best citizens. Margaret Lindeman was the wife of John Luther and mother of Martin; she was a woman commendable for all virtues beseeming a worthy matron, especially for her modesty, fear of God, and calling on his name, so that she was a pattern of virtue to many others.

---

[22] Thence Martin Luther went to Isenak.
Luther, *Epist. Tom. 1*, p.227

Martin Luther was born in Isleben, in the year of our Lord 1483, on November 10th at 9 o'clock at night, on St. Martin's Day, and was thence called *Martin*. His parents brought him up in the knowledge and fear of God, according to the capacity of his tender years, and taught him to read at home, and accustomed him to virtuous demeanor. The father of George Aemilius (as Luther often has related) first put him to school, where, though the truth was much darkened by clouds of popery, yet God preserved still the heads of catechism, the elements of the [Cisioian] grammar, some psalms, and forms of prayer.

At fourteen years of age, he – with John Reineck, who proved a man of special virtue and authority in those parts – was sent to Magdeburg, whence a league of entire friendship ever continued between these two, either because of a sympathy and agreement of their natures, or their education together in their first studies. At Magdeburg, he, as many others born of honest parents, lived a poor scholar for the space of one year. Thus even the greatest matters have small beginnings, and scarce anything is highly exalted but from a lowly degree.

Thence by his parents he was removed to Isenak, where was a school of great fame. Here was a schoolmaster, who (as Luther by experience found and would profess) taught grammar more dexterously and truly. One reason also of his being sent thither was because his mother was born there of a worthy and ancient family. There he perfected his grammar learning, and being of a very quick wit, and by nature fitted for eloquence, he soon surpassed his school-fellows in copiousness of speech and matter, and excelled in the expression of his mind both in prose and verse.

Upon this his tasting the sweetness of learning, he was inflamed with an earnest desire to go to some university, the wellspring of all good literature; and surely, if he had met with good and commendable tutors, he would – by his piercing wit – have attained all good arts, and perhaps he might by the milder studies of true philosophy, and diligence in well framing his style, somewhat have tempered the vehemence of his nature.

He went to Erford in the year 1501, where he fell upon the crabbed and thorny logic of that age, which he soon attained, as one who by the sagacity of his wit was better able to dive into the causes and other places of arguments than others.

Here, out of a desire for better learning, he read over Cicero, Livy, Virgil, and other monuments of ancient Latin authors. These he perused, not as a child, to glean phrases from them, but to discern what therein was useful towards the right conforming of man's life, and to that end seriously observed the counsels and grave sentences in those writers, and having a faithful and sure memory, whatever he read or heard, he had it still in readiness for present use. Hereby he so excelled in his youth, that the whole university admired his wit.

When at Erford he was graced with the degree of Master of Arts at twenty years of age, he read, as professor, Aristotle's physics, ethics, and other parts of philosophy. Afterward, his kindred, seeing it fit that such worthy endowments of wit and eloquence should be cherished for the public good, by their advice he betook himself to the study of the law. But not long after, when he was 21 years old, [all] of a sudden, besides the purpose of his parents and kindred (upon an affright from his faithful mate's violent death), he betook himself to the Augustinian monks college in Erford. But before he entered the monastery, he entertained his fellow students with a cheerful banquet and thereupon sent them letters valedictory; and sending to his parents the ring and gown of his degree of Master of Arts, unfolded to them the reason for the change of his course of life. It much grieved his parents that such excellent parts should be spent in a life little differing from death. But for a month's space no man could be admitted to speak with him.

Nor was it poverty, but the love of a pious life, which bent his mind to the monastical life, in which, though he spent his time in the usual school learning, and read the writers upon the *Sentences*,[23] and in public disputations clearly opened their inextricable labyrinths to the admiration of many, yet because in this kind of life he sought not to ennoble his fame, but to further his study of a pious life, he looked into those studies but upon the by, and with much ease attained their scholastical methods.

When on a time in the library of the college, running over the books thereof in order, he met with a copy of the Latin Bible, which he never saw before; there with admiration he observed that there were more evangelical and apostolical texts than what were read to the people in churches. In the Old Testament with great attention he read the story of Samuel and Hannah, his mother, and began to wish that he was the owner of a like book, which not long after he obtained. Hereupon he spent his time on the prophetical and apostolical writings, the fountains of all heavenly doctrine, seeking thence to inform his mind with God's will, and to nourish in himself the fear of God, and true faith in Christ from true and undoubted grounds. Some sickness and fear whet him on to attempt these studies more earnestly.

It is said that in this college Luther in his younger years fell into a most violent disease, insomuch that there was no hope of life; and that an ancient priest came to him, and with these words comforted him: "Sir, be of good courage,

---

[23] Peter Lombard's *Sentences*

for your disease is not mortal: God will raise you up to be a man who shall afford comfort to many others." At first, the monks handled him somewhat harshly, whilst he performed the Office of the Custos, and was compelled to cleanse the unclean places, as also to walk up and down the city with a bag or wallet. But upon the request of the university, of which he had been a member, he was eased of that burden.

He was often cheered up by conference with the ancient priest, to whom he revealed his fears and scruples of mind, and heard him discoursing of faith at large, and going on in the Creed, to the article "*I believe the remission of sins*," which he thus explained, namely, that a man must not only in general believe that sins are remitted to some men, as to David and to Esther, for this the devils believe, but that God commands that we should each man in particular believe that our sins are forgiven us in Christ Jesus.

"This exposition," said he, "is confirmed by St. Bernard, and showed him the place in his sermon upon the annunciation where these words are to be found. But add this, and believe this also, that thy sins are forgiven thee for Christ's sake. This is the testimony in thy heart, which the Spirit of God gives, saying, *Thy sins are forgiven thee*. For the apostle thus determines of the matter: That a man is freely justified by faith." Luther said that he was not only confirmed in the truth, but also put in mind of Saint Paul ever in these words, asserting this truth: *We are justified by faith.* Concerning this point, after he had read the expositions of diverse men, he further said that from the speeches of Paul, he observed to accrue unto himself much comfort, and great light to discern the vanity of other interpretations, which then were used.

Then he began to read St. Augustine's works, where both in his commentary on the Psalms, and in the book *Of The Spirit and Letter*, he found many evident places which confirmed this doctrine concerning faith and the comfort which was before kindled in his breast. Yet did he not utterly cast off the reading of Gabriel and Camaracensis, writers on the *Sentences*, but was able to recite them by heart in a manner. He spent much time in often reading Occam, and esteemed him for acuteness of wit before Thomas Aquinas and Scotus; also he studiously perused Gerson. But chiefly he read often Augustine's works and kept them well in memory. This earnest prosecution of his studies he began at Erford, and spent there five years in the college.

In the year 1507, he put on the priest's hood. The first mass which he celebrated was May 2, *Domini Cantate*. Then was he 24 years old. In this course he continued fifteen years, until the year of our Lord 1527. At that time John Staupicius, who endeavored to promote the university of Wittenberg lately begun, desired that the study of theology should there flourish, and well knew the wit and learning of Luther, and removed him to Wittenberg in the year 1508, when he was 26 years old.

Here in regard of his daily exercises in the schools and his sermons, the eminence of his good parts did more and more show themselves. And among other learned men, who attentively heard him, Martinus Mellurstad, commonly called *Lux Mundi*: *the light of the world*, often said of Luther that there was in him so noble a strain of wit, that he did verily presage that he would change the vulgar course of studies, which at that time was usual in schools, and prevailed.

At Wittenberg, Luther first explained Aristotle's logic and physics; yet intermitted not his study of divinity. Three years after, that is in the year 1510, he was sent into Italy and to Rome on behalf of his convent, for the deciding of some controversy among the monks. There he saw the pope, and the pope's palace, and the manners of the Roman clergy. Concerning which he says: "I was not long at Rome; there I said, and heard others say mass, but in that manner that, as often as I call them to mind, I detest them. For at the table I heard, among other matters, some courtesans laugh and boast, and some concerning the bread and wine on the altar to say: "Bread thou art, and bread thou shalt remain; Wine thou art, and wine thou shalt remain." He further adds that the priests celebrated the masses so hastily and perfunctorily, that he left off saying mass before he betook himself to the gospel and cried out: "Away with it, away with it."

In talk with his familiar friends, he would often rejoice at this his journey to Rome, and say that he would not for 1,000 florins have been without it. After his return from Rome, Staupicius so advising, he was made Doctor in Divinity, after the manner of the schools, and at the charge of Duke Frederick, Elector of Saxony. For the prince heard him preach, and admired the soundness of his invention, the strength of his arguments, and the excellence of the things which he delivered.

Now was Luther thirty years old, and had attained a maturity of judgment. Luther himself used to profess that he would have refused this honor, and that Staupicius would have him permit himself to be graced with this degree, saying pleasantly that there were many businesses in God's church wherein he would use Luther's help. This speech then spoken in a complimentary way at length proved true by the event. Thus many presages go before great changes. Soon after he began (as the place required) to explain the Epistle to the Romans and some Psalms, which he so cleared, that after a long and dark night, there seemed a new day to arise in the judgment of all pious and prudent men. Here he showed the difference of the law and gospel, and refuted an error then most frequent both in the schools and sermons, namely that men by their works can deserve remission of their sins, and that men are just before God by observing the discipline commanded, as the Pharisees taught.

Luther therefore recalled men's minds to the Son of God, and (as John Baptist) showed them the Lamb of God, who takes away the sins of the world, and taught them that for Christ's sake their sins are forgiven and that this benefit is received by faith. He cleared also other points of ecclesiastical truth. This beginning made him of great authority, and that much the more because his demeanor was suitable to his doctrine, so that his speech seemed to come from his heart, not from his lips only.

For the saying is as true as old: "A man's pious carriage makes his speech persuasive." Hence it was that men easily assented to him when afterward he changed some of their rites. As yet, he attempted not to do it, but was a rigid observer of good order, and added something more strict than usual. With the sweetness of this doctrine, all godly-minded men were enamored, and much it affected the learned, that Christ, the prophets, and apostles were brought out of darkness and prison, and that the difference of the Law and the Gospel, of God's Word and philosophy, (of which they read nothing in Thomas, Scotus, and their fellows) now was manifested. At this time also, young students were invited to a more exact study of the Latin and

Greek tongues, whereupon many worthy and ingenious men were much affected with the sweetness of polite learning and abhorred the barbarous and sophistical style of the monks. And now also Luther betook himself to the study of the Greek and Hebrew tongues, that upon his knowledge of the phrase and propriety of the original, he might more exactly judge of doctrines grounded thereupon.

Luther being thus busied into Misnia and Saxony, John Tecelius, a Dominican friar, brought indulgences to be sold. This Tecelius was adjudged to death by Maximilian the Emperor and commanded to be thrown into the river Oenoponte, but was pardoned at the request of Frederick, Duke of Saxony, who as it befell was in those coasts at his condemnation. This Tecelius averred (as other matters, so especially) that he had so large a commission from the pope, that though a man should have deflowered the Blessed Virgin, for money he could pardon the sin. And further he did not only give pardons for sins past, but for sins to come. And not long after an edict was set forth with Albertus the Archbishop's arms, which enjoined the officers in especial manner to commend the validity of the indulgences. The pardoners also at certain rates gave license on days prohibited to eat milk, cheese, eggs, and flesh [*meat*].

Luther's godly zeal being inflamed with these proceedings, set forth certain propositions concerning indulgences. These he publicly affixed at the church next to the Castle of Wittenberg, on All Saints' Eve, in the year 1517.

Hereupon Tecelius – persisting in his old course, and hoping thereby the more to oblige the pope to himself – called a senate of monks and divines of his own stamp and set them on work to write something against Luther. In the meantime he himself might not be silent, nor would he only preach against Luther, but with open mouth cried and thundered that Luther was deservedly to be burnt as a heretic, and also publicly cast Luther's propositions and his sermon concerning indulgences into the fire.

These violent courses of Tecelius and his accomplices necessarily put Luther upon a more copious declaration and defense of the Truth. Thus began these controversies, in which Luther aimed not at, nor so much as thought of the change which followed; nor indeed did altogether disallow of the indulgences, but desired a moderation in their use. Yea, it appeared that Luther would have been quiet, so that his adversaries had been enjoined silence. But when he saw that whatsoever the pope's crafty money-gatherers insinuated to Albertus, Archbishop of Mentz, was defended and believed by the common sort, and yet knew not that Tecelius was hired by Albertus to make those sermons for the purchasing of his bishop's robe, he – the day before the Calends of November, 1517 – complained to the

Archbishop by writing concerning their impious clamors, and entreated that he by the authority of his place would call in their libels, and prescribe to the preachers some other form of preaching their pardons – so Luther himself says.

At the same time, Luther sent him propositions concerning repentance and indulgences, which he then first set forth. These are extant in Tome 1 of Luther's works. The archbishop returned no answer to Luther's epistle. Tecelius opposed contrary positions made by Conrade Wimpin and others, at Frankfurt on Viadrus; and compared the pope with Peter, and the dross erected by the pope with Christ's dross.

At Halle in Saxony, the students of Wittenberg publicly burnt in the marketplace Tecelius's theses; of this Luther thus writes to John Longus: "That you may understand beforehand what was done about the burning of Tecelius's propositions, lest fame (as often it comes to pass) should misreport the matter.

The students being extremely weary of the old dunstical course of studies, and most desirous of the sacred Bible, and it may be out of their love to me, when they knew that one was sent by Tetzel to Halle, and was come with his positions, went presently unto him, and terrified him, asking him how he dared bring such stuff thither. Some bought [from] him, some took the rest from him, and (giving intimation that whosoever would see Tecelius' positions burnt should come to the marketplace at two o'clock) burnt 800 of them. All this was unknown to the prince, the senate, the rector, and all of us. This great injury done the man by our students displeases myself and the rest.

And though I am blameless, yet I fear that the whole proceeding will be laid to my charge. A great bruit was raised hereupon, but especially among them, with a just indignation. What will be the issue hereof, I cannot say; sure it is that my danger will be much the more."

When Luther perceived that the positions were very well liked of, and entertained as sound and orthodox, which he at first propounded to be discussed by disputation, till the church defined what was to be thought concerning indulgences, he wrote to Jerome, Bishop of Brandenburg, under whose jurisdiction he was, and submitted what he had written to the bishop's judgment; and entreated him that he would dash out with his pen, or consume with the fire, what he thought unsound. The bishop answered Luther and declared that his desire was that the setting forth of his arguments about those matters should a little while be deferred, and that he wished that the common talk about indulgences had never been. Luther answered: "I am content so to do, and had rather obey than work miracles, if I could well do them." He wrote also to John Staupicius, the vicar of the Augustinian party, and gave him an account of his proceedings, and sent to him the answers of the disputations concerning the validity of indulgences to be imparted to Pope Leo X. In these he showed the pope how inconsiderately and sordidly the disposers of his indulgences had abused his authority. He also annexed thereunto the protestation, which is extant in the first tome of his works.

Now also John Eckius opposed Luther's conclusions with *Obelisks* or *Marks of Disgrace*. To them Luther opposed his *Asterisks* or *Notes of Approbation*. After this, Silvester Prierias, a Dominican, and master of (as they call it) the sacred palace, very confidently entered into the quarrel with a dialogue and preface to Leo the Pope. In this writing, Prierias set down certain theses for the ground of his judgment. Luther answered him and opposed the sacred Scripture to the authority of Thomas Aquinas, whom Prierias cited. Upon this, a reply was made against Luther. In it, Prierias said that he liked it well that Luther did submit himself to the pleasure of the pope, was not ambitious, and did defend Thomas as the angelic doctor. Luther answered this with an epistle only to the reader, and together with other matters, said: "If the pope and cardinals are of the same opinion, if at Rome the same doctrine is taught, there is no doubt, but that Rome is the very seat of Antichrist, and that Greece, and Bohemia, and all others are happy, that they made a departure from the pope," and that new commendations of the pope were daily invented to prevent the calling of a lawful council.

Afterwards, John Hogostratus, a Dominican, writes bitterly against Luther, and excites the pope to use the rounder course of fire and faggot. Luther answered him in brief and told him of his cruel bent and wittily taxed the ignorance of the man, and admonished him not to proceed to seek *laureolam in mustaceo*: the laurel garland in so mean a perfection.

In the year 1518 Luther, though most men dissuaded him, yet to show his observance of authority, went (for the most part on foot) to the college of Heidelberg. At Herbipolis the Bishop entertained him courteously. So also did Wolfgang, the Count Palatine at Heidelberg. In the College of the Augustinians now called *the College of Sapience*, he disputed about justification by faith. Bucer was there present, and by his quickness in writing took what Luther spoke, and imparted all to Beatus Rhenanus, who gave Luther much deserved commendations.

Of this disputation, Luther thus speaks: "The doctors admitted my disputing with them willingly, and argued the matter with me with much modesty, that in that very regard, I hold them worth much commendations. For though they thought that divinity strong, yet they all argued seriously and strongly against it, except one alone, who was the fifth of them a junior doctor; he made all the auditory to laugh by saying, if the rustic [root] should hear this, they would stone and kill us."

Upon Luther's return, he wrote an epistle to Judocus, a divine and philosopher of Isenac, once his tutor, where he has this speech: "All the doctors of Wittenberg (in the doctrine concerning grace and good works) are of my judgment – yea, the whole university except one licentiate doctor, Sebastian; even the prince himself and our ordinary bishop, and many of the chieftains, and all the ingenious citizens with joint consent affirm, that before they neither knew, nor heard of the gospel, nor of Christ."

After that he put forth in print the resolutions and declarations of his propositions about indulgences, which he dedicated to Pope Leo X, as was before said. The causes of his printing them were, as he said: to mitigate his adversaries, to satisfy some men's request, and not to suffer some to conceive that the whole business was determined. For he confessed that of many things he yet doubted, of some things he was ignorant, and did pertinaciously affirm nothing; but did humbly submit all to the pope's determination. Hereupon Maximilian the Emperor – being solicitous of the event of disputations of this nature – moved the pope to interpose his own authority. The pope by Cardinal Thomas Cajetan cited Luther to Rome. This he also desired of Frederick, Elector of Saxony. Luther having notice hereof, mainly endeavored that the cause might be handled in Germany under competent judges; and at length he prevailed, by the mediation of Wittenberg University to the pope, and by Charles Miltitius, a German, the pope's chamberlain, and the mediation of the Elector of Saxony to Cajetan – then the pope's legate – that at Augsburg before the legate himself, Luther might plead his own cause.

About the beginning of October, Luther came on foot to Augsburg, in his hood borrowed [from] Wenceslaus Linck, and much wearied with the journey; and upon assurance of his safety was admitted to the cardinal's presence, who admonished him firstly to become a sound member of the church, and to recant the errors which he had divulged; secondly, to promise that he would not again teach his former doctrines; thirdly, that he would abstain from other doctrines which would disturb the peace of the church. Here also it was objected to him that he denied the merit of Christ to be a treasure of indulgences; and that he taught that faith was necessary for all who should come to the sacrament. Cajetan proved his own opinion by the decree of Clement VI, and at large extolled the authority of the See of Rome, as being falsely preferred before all Scriptures and councils.

After much debating of the matters, Luther entreated some time to deliberate thereon, and returned the next day, and in the presence of some witnesses and a scribe, and four of the emperor's counselors, professed that he gave the church of Rome all due observance, and if he had spoken anything dissenting from the judgment of the church, he would reverse it; but could revoke no error, being not yet convicted by Scripture of any, and did appeal to the judgment of the church.

Hereupon the legate, sharply chiding Luther, dismissed him, and dealt with Staupicius to bring Luther to revoke what he had taught. But Luther, not convinced as yet by Scripture, persisted in the truth. Yet at length fearing lest the cardinal should make more use of his power and greatness than [scholastic]-like disputations, he appealed to Rome and departed from Augsburg on October 20th, because the cardinal charged him not to come into his presence unless he would recant. Yet Luther left behind him an epistle to the cardinal and affixed thereto a formal appeal unto the pope.

Cajetan took Luther's departure in ill part, and wrote to the Duke of Saxony that he would either send Luther to Rome, or banish him out of his territories, and entreats him not to give credit to Luther's defenders, and to take heed of staining the illustrious family whence he was descended. The elector returned [the] answer that now it was not in his power to do this, because Luther was not convicted of any error, and did much good service in the university, and did offer his cause to trial and disputation. The resolution of the Duke was more confirmed by an epistle of Erasmus, and the intercession and vote of the University of Wittenberg.

Here I may not pass over a notable proof of Luther's heroic courage. When Luther came to Augsburg, he – by the counsel of such as the Prince Elector sent with him – waited three days to have the emperor's letters for his safety. In the meantime, the cardinal sent one for Luther; but he denied to come until the Emperor granted what he desired. At this, the messenger was offended and said: "Do you think that Prince Frederick will take up arms [on] your behalf?" "I desire it not, said Luther, in any wise. Then the party; where then will you abide? Luther answered: "Under the cope of heaven." The Italian replied: "Had you the pope and the cardinals in your power, what would you do?" "I would," said Luther, "give them all due honor and reverence." At this the messenger, after the Italian manner [of] biting his thumbs, went away.

Upon these dealings, Luther's spirit fainted not, yet lest he should cause detriment or danger to any one, or derive suspicion on his prince, and that he might more freely deal with the papal crew, would have gone into France or some other country. But his friends, on the contrary, counseled him to stick firmly to Saxony; and that the pope's legate should be certified that Luther was ready in any safe place appointed him to make his answer. But Luther – having settled his resolution to depart – took his leave of the prince elector, and by a letter sent to him on November 29th, thanked his Highness for all friendly offices of his love. The prince sent that letter to the legate, and appointed Luther to abide at Wittenberg.

Of this, Luther thus wrote: "The prince was fully minded that I should stay; but what his mind now is, since the royal proceedings are published, and I have appealed to the council, I know not."

For he – understanding by the cardinal's letter that judgment should pass on him at Rome – made a new appeal, saying that he was forced of necessity to appeal from the pope to the council ensuing; which was in many respects to be preferred before the pope.

About the same time towards the end of the 18th year, the pope sent Charles Miltitius, a Misnian Knight, and bestowed on Prince Frederick a golden rose, according to custom consecrated by the pope on the fourth Sunday in Lent, and exhorted him to continue in the faith of his ancestors. He was earnest with Luther to be reconciled to the pope, and had seventy apostolic briefs (as they call them) to show that if the prince would deliver him out of his custody, for which cause the pope sent him the rose, in seventy towns the seventy briefs should be set up, and so he should be brought safe to Rome.

But he opened the closet of his heart to Luther himself, when he thus spoke: "O Martin, I conceived you to be an old man, and sitting in some solitary place as an ancient divine, in some private manner to have disputed your tenets: but now I see you to be in your best age, and full of vigor. Had I 25,000 armed men I could not be confident that I could bring you to Rome; for as I came hitherward, I tried how men stood affected, and found that where one man stood for the pope, three stood for you against him."

What Miltitius did in this kind was ridiculous, for he asked of women and maids in the inns as he came, what they thought of the seat of Rome. They – not knowing the force of this speech – answered, "What know we, whether at Rome ye sit on wooden or stone seats?" He further required of Luther that he would have a regard to the church's peace; and promised to endeavor that the pope should do the like. Luther freely promised most readily to do whatever he could with a safe conscience in regard of God's truth, and affirmed that himself was desirous and studious of peace, and that it was not his fault that these stirs arose; for necessity had urged him to do what he had done.

Miltitius also called unto him Tecelius, the chief [originator] of these debates; and with sharp words and threats so daunted the man, until now a clamorous, unaffrighted, bold face, terrible to all, so that ever after he languished and with heart's grief pined away. Luther wrote a consolatory letter to him in this case; but for fear of the pope's indignation he died. Frederick the Elector, a prudent and religious prince, neither yielded to the pope's desire, nor vouchsafed his rose any respect, though Miltitius wonderfully boasted of it at Dresden, and said: "Doctor Martin is in my power." About this time, the Bohemians – sending a book written by John Hus to Luther – encouraged him to constancy and patience, and confessed that the divinity taught by Luther was sound and right.

Matters being grown to this height of dispute, and Luther having many adversaries; at Leipzig, a town in Misnia belonging to George Duke of Saxony, cousin-german to Prince Frederick, in the 19th year a disputation was held. Thither came Andreas Carolostadius accompanied with Luther, Melanchthon, and Barninus Duke of Pomerania. He at that time was in office in the University of Wittenberg. Thither came also John Eckius, a divine of Ingolstadt.

Hereupon the 17th day of June, John Eckius and Carolostadius began the disputation about free will, namely: whether there is in man any free will to do good as of himself? that is, as they say: whether in congruity we deserve grace, when we do what is in us to do? Eckius granted that there is not in man a genuine and natural power and ability to do a good work, but an acquired

[one]. On this point eight days were spent by his playing the sophister.

Luther could by no means obtain leave of Duke George freely with his safety to dispute, and thereupon came not as a disputer, but as an auditor to Leipzig, under the protection granted to Carolostadius. Whereupon Eckius coming to Luther's lodging said that he heard that Luther refused to dispute, Luther answered: "How can I dispute, seeing I cannot obtain protection from George the Duke?" To this Eckius replied: "If I may not dispute with you, I will no longer dispute with Carolostadius. For I came hither to dispute with you. If I can obtain for you the Duke's leave, will you dispute?" When Luther assented thereto, Eckius presently procured for him a public grant of safety and liberty to dispute. This Eckius did out of an assured confidence of victory and renown to himself, by confirming that the pope is the head of the church, *jure divino*, by divine right: which Luther denied. Hence Eckius took occasion at large to flatter the pope and demerit his favor, and to derive much hatred and envy on Luther. This the bold champion stoutly attempted in the whole disputation, but was not able to make good his cause or confute Luther. Eckius' chief arguments were: that the church could not be without a head, seeing it was a body consisting of several members.

Then he produced the place in Matthew: "Thou art Peter," etc., and some speeches of St. Jerome and Cyprian, and the Council of Constance, where against the Articles of the Hussites, it was concluded that it was necessary to salvation that men should believe that the pope was the ecumenical bishop, or Christ's vicar over the whole world. Afterwards, they entered into dispute about Purgatory and indulgences, (but in brief) about repentance, about remission both of sin and its punishment, and about the power of priests.

The two last days Carolostadius disputed again, and on the 14th day of July the disputation ended. This disputation was set forth afterward by Luther, who granted that the pope by human right was head of the church. Whereupon Duke George – inviting Luther and Eckius to dinner, and embracing both of them – said: "Whether the pope has his authority by divine or human right, pope he is." Luther afterward changed his opinion about this point. Before this disputation at Leipzig, Luther was desired by Charles Miltitius to go to Confluence, there to plead his cause before him being the pope's commissary. But Luther excused himself, and showed that for many reasons, he neither could, nor ought to go thither.

In the year 1520, upon Miltitius's advice, Luther wrote to the pope, and sent him his book lately written concerning Christian liberty, and offered conditions of peace. About this time, Frederick the Elector fell into a grievous sickness. Whereupon Luther, moved by some friends, and out of Christian charity, wrote the book called *Tesseradecades* to comfort him. Then also he wrote the book *Of Confession of Sins*, in which he took occasion to speak of vows, and deplored their torturing of men's consciences. And whereas in another treatise written by him, he had said that he judged it behooveful if the council would so permit that the Lord's Supper should be administered to all in both kinds; this speech, because it directly crossed the last Lateran Council, was excepted against by many: amongst whom was John Bishop of Misnia, who prohibited the churchmen under his jurisdiction to administer the Lord's Supper in both kinds, and enjoined them to suppress Luther's book. Luther maintained his cause and answered his edict.

In the meantime, the divines of Louvain (consulting with Adrian Cardinal of Tortosa, then in Spain) and the divines of Cologne by a decree censured some of Luther's books as wicked and worthy to be burnt, and held it fit that Luther should recant his opinions. When Luther heard of this, he answered every particular punctually. And because he found so many and so great adversaries, he wrote to Charles V, newly created Emperor, and entreating pardon for this his address, humbly besought him that he would so long only afford him protection, as that he might give account of his proceedings, and overcome or be overcome: because it would well beseem the Imperial power not to permit the innocent to be violently handled and trampled on by their wicked adversaries.

To the same purpose he wrote to other dukes and lords of the empire, and showed them how he began and was drawn into these attempts. Not long after he wrote to Albertus Archbishop of Mentz, Cardinal, and in submissive manner showed how he was condemned by two sorts of men; one who never read his books; the other, who read them, but with hearts full of hatred and prejudice. The bishop answered that he heartily desired that all sacred matters should be handled both by Luther and all other divines (as it was meet) religiously, reverently, modestly, without tumults, envy, or contumely. He said moreover that it was a grief to him to hear that some great men disputed concerning the primacy of Rome, free will, and other slight matters (so he called them) not much pertaining to a Christian indeed; and that such like rash opinions could not be broached among the ignorant people but with encouraging them to disobedience.

He wrote also about the Lord's Supper's celebrating in both kinds, and about the authority of councils. And shut up his letter with Gamaliel's verdict: "If thy work be of God; it will stand firm and immovable; if it was begun of envy or pride, it will easily be blown away." In like manner, Luther wrote to Adolphus, Bishop of Mersberg, who answered him to the same purpose, and admonished him that he would overrule his pen with the love of Christ the Author of our peace.

At the same time it befell that Frederick, Duke of Saxony, had some occasion to send to Rome, and gave the business in charge to Valentine Dithleben, a German. He brought word back that the Elector was in disgrace at Rome for Luther's sake because he permitted his new opinions to be dispersed. The prince hereupon thus wrote in his own defense, and answered that he never defended the doctrine and books of Luther, nor was of that bent; and though he did hear that many learned men approved Luther's judgment, yet he opened not his mind therein.

Further, he said that Luther was ready to give an account of his doctrine before the pope's legate, so that he might be assured of safe conduct: and that if his error was detected, he would change his opinion: and that Luther of his own accord would have departed out of those coasts, had not Miltitius persuaded to detain him there, rather than to permit him to settle elsewhere, that so he might more freely and safely attempt some higher design. And therefore that there was no cause why any one should have an ill opinion of him.

To this letter the pope returned answer, and sending a copy of the bull which Eckius had obtained, desired that the Elector would make Luther to recant, or if he refused so to do, he would imprison him and keep him safe until he further declared his pleasure. At this the Court of Saxony was somewhat troubled, and Luther began to think of some retired place, where he might conceal himself. Some noble Germans, approvers of Luther's judgment, hearing this, offered Luther entertainment and protection, as namely, Francis Sickingen, Ulrich von Hutten, Sylvester de Schavenburgen – of whom the said Sylvester wrote to Luther, and entreated him, not to depart into Bohemia, or into any other country, but to come to him, during the time of the pope's exasperation and menaces, and promised that a hundred French [horsemen] should attend his safety.

Hereupon Luther – taking courage – admonished Spalatinus that this course should by the letter of Duke Frederick, be made known to the cardinal of St. George.

These are Luther's words: "I send you the letter of Sylvester Schavenb. the French knight, and were it not displeasing to you, I desire that by the letter of the prince, notice may be given to the Cardinal of St. George, whereby they may know that should they with their threats and curses expel me from Wittenberg, they should effect nothing else but to make a bad matter much worse. For now there are not only in Bohemia, but even in the midst of Germany, such princes who both will and can defend me from the threats thundered out against me by my adversaries. And then perhaps it may so fall out that abiding under their protection, I shall more strongly bend my forces against the Romanists than if under the princes' government, I should publicly perform my place as reader of divinity. This, unless God prevents it, will doubtless be the issue of this matter.

Hitherto I have given all due respect to the prince, but then, if I am provoked by ill usage, I shall not need to submit unto him. And therefore in what matters soever I have not so roughly dealt with them, let them attribute my forbearance therein not to my modesty, nor to their tyranny, nor their deserts, but to my respect to the prince and to his authority, as also to the common good of the students of Wittenberg.

Concerning myself, I venture upon the danger, and contemn Rome's both fury and favor. Let them censure and burn all mine, I will not be reconciled to them, nor at any time hereafter join with them. On the contrary I (unless I can get no fire) will burn all the pontifical law, the sink of heresies; yet I will put an end to my humble observance, which I have hitherto in vain showed; and wherewith the enemies of the gospel are more and more incensed."

Luther also, before he saw the pope's bull, put forth his book *Of The Babylonian Captivity*, in which he wished that what he had written concerning indulgences was abolished, and this proposition divulged in its stead: "Indulgences are the wicked tricks of Rome's flatterers." And instead of what he wrote against the pope, [he offered] this proposition: "The papacy is a robustious hunting practiced by the Bishop of Rome." Then he handled the sacraments, and acknowledged but three of the seven to be sacraments of Christ's covenant. He wrote also against the "execrable bull of Antichrist," called the pope *Antichrist*, and confirmed the articles censured by the bull.

Charles the Emperor that year came to Aquisgran, where with great solemnity he was crowned emperor. About the Calends of September, he with Frederick, Elector of Saxony went to Colonia Agrippina. At this time, the controversies of religion being hotly prosecuted, the elector would not suddenly do anything of his own head in a matter of so great import, but would try the votes of the most prudent and learned clerks, including Erasmus, whom he sent for from Leuven to Cologne.

When he first asked Erasmus' judgment concerning Luther and wondered that so great and extreme extreme hatred should be raised by some monks and the pope against Luther, whose life and carriage he deemed to be commendable, and doctrine not impious, Erasmus answered in a pleasant manner: that his Highness "need not wonder at that, for Luther, in his disputations, dealt against the monks' bellies and the pope's crown." Afterwards, seriously and gravely giving his opinion concerning the controversies of these times, he showed that indulgences and other abuses and superstitions were justly taxed, and that their reformation was necessary, and that the sum of Luther's doctrine was orthodox, and that only he seemed too vehement and violent in contending with his adversaries, and that an evangelical business was to be handled after an evangelical manner.

Frederick the Elector, being confirmed in the truth by the sage judgment of Erasmus, did gravely admonish advised Luther to moderate his fierceness in disputes. Then also there came to Cologne Martin Caracciolo and Jerome Alexander, who again set upon Duke Frederick in the pope's name. But when the elector's response was not as they had hoped, they said that they must deal with him according to the form of the decree, and burned Luther's books.

It is reported that these advocates of the pope did promise Erasmus a bishopric of rich revenue, if he would write against Luther. But he answered: "That Luther was a man too great for him to write against, and that he learned more from one short page of Luther's writings than from all Thomas Aquinas books.

It is also said that Margaret the Emperor's aunt, who ruled all Belgium, when the *magistri nostri* of Leuven complained that Luther with his writings did subvert all

Christendom did demand what manner a man Luther was, when they answered that he was an unlearned monk, she replied: "Why then, see that all you learned men, being a great multitude, write against that one unlearned fellow; and doubtless the world will give more credit to many of you being learned than to him being but one and unlearned."

Luther, knowing what was done with his writings, on December 10th 1520 called the students of Wittenberg together, and in a frequent assembly of learned men, before the gate of Elster near to the great college, where a fire was made, cast the pope's laws and the bull of Leo with some writings of Eckius, Emser, and others therein, and said: "Because thou troublest Christ the holy one of God, eternal fire will trouble thee."

The next day, he expounded the Psalms, and earnestly charged his auditors that as they loved the salvation of their souls, they should take heed of the pope's statutes. And in writing gave a reason presently of this his action. And out of the great multitude of errors in the pope's laws culled out these thirty:

(1) The pope and his clergy are not bound to be subject and obedient to the commandments of God.

(2) It is not a precept but a counsel of St. Peter, where he says that all men ought to be subject to kings.

(3) That by the sun, the papal power; and by the moon, the imperial or secular power in a commonwealth were signified.

(4) That the pope and his chair were not bound to be subject to councils and decrees.

(5) That the pope had in the closet of his breast all laws, and plenary power over all laws.

(6) Whence it follows that the pope has power to disannul, to change and determine of all councils, and all constitutions and ordinances, as he daily practices.

(7) That the pope of Rome has a right to require an oath of all bishops, and to oblige them to him in regard of their palls received [from] him.

(8) If the pope is so neglectful of his own and his brethren's salvation, and so unprofitable and remiss in his place, that he carry along with himself (as if he was the chief slave of hell) innumerable people to be eternally tormented, [then] no mortal man ought to reprove him for this sin.

(9) That the salvation of all faithful men depends on the pope, next after God.

(10) No man on earth can judge the pope, or censure his determinations; but the pope is judge of all men.

(11) The See of Rome gives authority to all rights and laws, and is itself subject to none of them.

(12) The rock upon which Christ in Matthew 16, builds his church is the See of Rome, with them adjoining.

(13) The keys were given to Saint Peter only.

(14) Christ's priesthood was translated from him to Saint Peter.

(15) The pope has power to make ordinances and laws for the Catholic Church.

(16) This sentence: "*Whatsoever thou bindest on earth, shall also be bound in heaven*," establishes this conclusion: that the pope has power to charge the catholic church even with his rash laws.

(17) That his command of abstinence from flesh, eggs, butter, and other meats made of milk, is to be observed, else men sin and are liable to excommunication.

(18) The pope forbidding all priests to marry wives, inhibits all the priesthood from matrimony.

(19) Pope Nicholas (either III or IV) in his Antichristian decretal, among other matters badly decreed, well judged that Christ by giving the keys gave power over both the celestial and terrestrial kingdom.

(20) The pope judges that loud and impious lie for a truth, and requires that it is received, namely, that Constantine the Great gave him the Roman provinces and countries and power over the whole inferior world.

(21) The pope affirms that he is the heir of the sacred Roman Empire. *De Sententia Et Re Judicata, c. Pastoralis*.

(22) The pope teaches that it is just and lawful for a Christian by force to repulse force and violence.

(23) That inferiors and subjects may be disobedient and resist their princes, and that the pope can depose kings.

(24) The pope labors to have power to dissolve and break all oaths, leagues, [and] obligations made between superiors and inferiors.

(25) The pope has power to break and alter vows made to God. *De vot. et vot. red*.

(26) The pope teaches that he that delays to pay his vow commanded by God, is not to be censured, as a breaker of his vow. *Ibid*.

(27) The pope teaches that no married man or woman can serve God.

(28) The pope compares his unprofitable laws with the gospels and sacred Scriptures.

(29) The pope has power to interpret and unfold or expound the sacred Scripture at his pleasure and will: and to permit no man to interpret the same otherwise than the pope himself pleases.

(30) The pope receives not his authority, power, strength, and dignity from the Scripture; but the Scripture from the pope.

This in brief is the sum of the whole canon law: *the pope is God on earth, supreme in all heavenly, earthly, spiritual, and secular matters.* And: *all things are the pope's; to whom none dare say: what [are you doing]?*

Here Frederick Prince Elector obtained [permission from] the emperor to call Luther to the court held at Worms in March in the year 1521. Luther – receiving the emperor's grant for his safety – went from Wittenberg, and was conducted thence by Casparus Sturm, herald, and accompanied with Justus Jonas, Jerome Schurf, and Nicolas Amsdorf. Of the students, he took only Peter Suavenus, a Dane, as his companion, who afterward, being called by Christian, King of Denmark to his court, did much advance good letters, and did the church good service. When he came to Heidelberg, he proffered to dispute publicly with any that would.

Here many did dehort Luther from going to Worms. Others said that by the burning of his books, he might know what was the pope's censure concerning himself. Others told him of the usage of Huss and Savonarola. But Luther, with a resolute courage, lightly regarded their advice, and said that these discouragements were but cast into his way by Satan, who knew that by the profession of the truth, especially in so illustrious a place, his kingdom would be shaken and damaged. He further broke forth into these words: "If I knew that there were so many devils at Worms, as tiles on the houses, yet would I go thither."

Also Francis of Sickingen, one in high esteem with the emperor, at Bucer's request did invite Luther to come to his castle at Ebernburg, where the cause might more commodiously be agitated. But Luther answered that he was sent for by the emperor, not to Ebernburg, but to Worms; and thither he would go. So taking his journey he came to Worms on April 6th, which was the third holy day after Misericordias Domini. They say the Duke of Bavaria's jester – whether suborned by others, or by some instinct – met Luther at his entrance into the town with a cross, as is wont in funerals, and sung with a loud voice: "Welcome comest thou hither, and much desired of us, who sat in darkness." Presently some counseled Caesar, that Luther was to be dealt with as they did with Hus. But Caesar thought it just to make good his promise: and especially Louis the Elector Palatine withstood the design, and prudently said that if they should take that course with Luther, it would set a brand of infamy and eternal disgrace on the name of Germany.

On the 17th day of April, at 4 o'clock in the afternoon, he appeared before the emperor, and many princes, his assessors. Here John Eckius, a lawyer, Caesar's spokesman, and official of Triers, upon command said, with an audible voice: "Martin Luther, there are two causes, why Caesar, with the consent of the princes and states, have sent for you: which I now propound to you, and expect your answer. First, whether these books (here he held up a bundle of books written in the Latin and German tongues) were written by you, and do you acknowledge them to be yours? The second, whether you will revoke and recant anything in them, or stand in defense of them."

Jerome Schurf – a lawyer on Luther's part – desired that the titles of the books might be recited and spoken publicly, which being done, Luther briefly repeated what was desired of him, and answered: "Concerning the books now named, I profess and acknowledge that they be mine; but concerning my defense of what I have written (that I may answer rightly thereunto) seeing it is a matter of very great moment [*importance*], I desire (that I may not speak rashly and against my conscience) some time to deliberate."

After some debate of the matter, Eckius said again: "Though by Caesar's letters missive, you might well understand the cause, why you were sent for, and therefore need not to delay, but make your answer presently; yet Caesar, such is his clemency, grants you one day to deliberate on the matter: and commands that tomorrow about this hour you here present yourself, and make your distinct answer by word of mouth, and not by writing."

Upon Luther's desiring of respite, some thought that he would not be constant, but they failed in their opinion. Here I may not pass it over in silence, that when Luther drew near to Caesar's throne, many of the princes' counsel encouraged him, saying: that he should be of good courage and not faint, nor fear them who could kill the body only, but not hurt the soul. Others put him in mind to meditate on this: "When ye shall appear before kings and princes, be not solicitous, how and what to answer. For in that moment, it shall be given you, what you shall say."[24]

The day following, Luther appeared at the hour appointed. And after that Eckius had asked him *what now was his resolution?*, he first humbly desired of the emperor and princes that they would grant him their gentle attention, and then said:

"Of the books which I have written, some of them tend to faith and piety; to these my adversaries give ample testimony. Should I recant these, I might be justly censured as a wicked man. Others of my books are against the pope of Rome and papistical doctrine, which both has and still does much trouble the Christian world, and does much mischief. These, should I revoke, I should confirm their tyranny. The third sort of my books are against some private men, who defend the papists' cause, and by many calumnies upon me. In these, I confess, I have been too vehement; and besides, I confess that I am not of an unerring perfection. But yet I cannot safely revoke these books, unless I will set open a gap to the impudency of

---

[24] Matthew 10:19-20

many. Being a man, I may err, and therefore desire anyone better to instruct me by the testimony of Scripture."

When he had thus said, Eckius, with a sour countenance, replied. "You answer not to the matter, nor does it pertain to you to call the authority of the council into question. A plain and direct answer is required of you, whether you desire that your writings should stand good."

Then said Luther: "Seeing you, O Caesar, and the princes command me to answer punctually, I obey. This is my resolution: Unless I am convicted by testimony of Scripture or evident reason, I may not revoke anything which I have written or spoken. For I will not in any wise wound my conscience. I do not conform my belief to the pope's or the councils' determinations alone; for they have often erred and delivered contrarieties one to another. I neither can nor will do anything concerning God's Word to the offense of my conscience, seeing as it is neither safe nor honest to do anything against conscience. This will I stand to: vary from this I may not. God help me, Amen."

When he was again urged, he persisted in this answer. So they departed. The next day Caesar sent a letter to the assembly of the princes; this was the sum thereof: "Our ancestors and other Christian princes obeyed carefully the church of Rome which now Dr. Martin Luther opposes. Now because he is resolute not to yield one inch of his errors, we cannot without a blemish to our name depart from the example of our ancestors, but must defend the ancient faith, and be assistant to the See of Rome. We will then excommunicate Martin Luther himself and all his adherents, and take any other course, which may conduce to extinguish these disputes. But we will not in any wise violate, and break our promise made to him under our seal, but give him safe conduct to the place, whence he came."

This letter of Caesar was diligently and a good while scanned in the senate by the princes. It is reported that some there were among those who would have followed the decree and practice of the council of Constance, and held themselves not bound to make good the promise of his safe return. But some of the princes, especially Louis, Prince Palatine (as it is reported) earnestly withstood them. Wherefore they judged that not only fidelity was to be observed towards him, but also, that he was not rashly to be condemned, because the matter was of very great consequence, whatsoever the Emperor decreed – whom being newly come to the imperial seat, they did well perceive to be pressed and provoked by the pope's instruments against Luther.

After a few days, the Archbishop of Trier and other princes, who by Caesar's permission were present, called Luther on April 24th unto them. The bishop then in a friendly manner dealt with him to desist from his resolution. But Luther – giving him thanks for care of his safety – stood firmly in his former doctrine, and submitted what even he had written to Caesar's and the princes' perusal and judgment, so that they tried them by God's word.

When the bishop asked him what remedy he knew or could advise for these stirs, Luther answered: "None other than that of Gamaliel in the Acts of the Apostles. If this counsel and proceeding be of men, it will not continue; if of God, no power of man can dissolve it." And this he besought him to signify to the pope.

The bishop again said: "What if the articles were collected and submitted to the council?" Luther answered, "Yes they might, so that they were not the same which the council at Constance condemned." The bishop replying that he feared they would be the very same, Luther courageously answered: "Those will I defend, though I was presently to die." Hereupon the bishop quietly dismissed Luther: who entreated him, that he might have leave to return to his friends, and have safe conduct from Caesar. The bishop promised to obtain it for him, and a little while after sent Eckius, the officer of Caesar, to signify to Luther that he had free liberty to depart under Caesar's protection within 21 days; also he was bid not to preach in his journey home, nor to write anything, which might raise further stirs. Luther answered: "As it seems good to the Lord, so be it; blessed be the name of God." Afterward he gave humble thanks to Caesar and the princes, and commended himself to them.

On the 26th of April, Luther taking his leave departed from Worms, Caspar Sturm, a messenger, some hours after followed him, and found him at Oppenheim. Luther, being in his journey, sent letters back both to Caesar and the princes electors, and states of the empire, commending himself and his cause to them; and said he was ready to do anything, which was meet, except to revoke anything that he knew to be warranted by God's Word.

The Emperor hereupon, on May 28th, proscribed Luther: whom Pope Leo – on the 28th of March on the day of the administration of the Lord's Supper – had excommunicated. At this all men stood earnestly expecting what those thunderbolts would effect.

Frederick the Elector, a prudent prince, seeing Luther to have incurred the hatred of all. [So] that no danger might seize on him, committed the business of conveying Luther into some safe place, where he might be free from access, to some faithful friends of the nobility, that there he should be kept private, until Caesar was departed out of Germany, they presently, faithfully, and secretly conveyed him to the Castle of Wartburg near Isenach. This place Luther afterward used to call his Patmos. There were but eight privy to this, who did it with that secrecy that not any but themselves could know what was become of him. It is reported that the papists set their wizards on work to descry him; but they could not certainly design the place where he was. Luther abode in that woody wilderness about ten months, and in this retiredness wrote diverse useful treatises for the church; as the explications of the gospels and epistles dedicated to Albertus of Mansfield, and the book against Latomus about sin remaining in the regenerate. Besides, he cut in two the two sinews of the pope's kingdom, namely, private masses and monastic vows, which books he dedicated to the Augustinian friars (who in his absence abrogated private masses and began to dispute about monastic vows) and to his father.

They of Wittenberg also gave a reason to the elector why they did so, and showed to what end temples and colleges were instituted at the first, that is: not for private Masses, but that young people might be there brought up piously, and that the means they were endowed with, were for the use of both readers and scholars that were in want. And that this buying and selling of masses was crept in within 400 years of that time.

Luther found courteous entertainment and kind respect in that his wilderness, for in his epistles, he often mentions the friendly offices of his host, to whom he preached on the Lord's Day and at festival times in his private chapel. Sometimes Luther for his health's sake went forth into the strawberry groves, and somewhat further into the monasteries, which were near, taking upon him the name Junker George, a nobleman, and accompanied only with one attendant, who was faithful and secret, and would often warn Luther in the places where they were entertained, not presently to lay aside his sword, and to take in hand the books before him; for so he might be descried.

Sometimes he went forth a-hunting with his friends. Of this sport thus he writes:

"I was a-hunting two days, to see that lordly but bittersweet sport. Here we took two hares, and some silly young partridges. The sport is meet for such as have nothing else to do. There did I contemplate as a divine amidst their nets and dogs. Nor did the outward appearance of the game more delight me than what I conceived by it moved me to pity and grief. For what could this sport signify and resemble, but by the dogs, wicked Popish divines, and by the nets, the cunning tricks and wiles by which they seek to catch harmless Christians, as hunters [do] those silly creatures? This was a most evident mystery of the pursuing of plain-hearted and faithful souls.

Yet was there a more cruel mystery presented to me: when by my means, we kept a young hare alive, and put her in my coat's sleeve, and so left her. In the meantime, the dogs finding it, broke one of her legs, and taking her by the as she was in the sleeve, stopped her wind. Thus it is with Satan and the pope, who cruelly destroy poor souls without regard of my pains to save them. I was by this time weary of this sport, and thought that more pleasing, where bears, wolves, boars, foxes, and such like savage creatures are struck dead with darts and arrows. It comforted me again, (for I took it as a mystery and resemblance of salvation) that hares and harmless creatures are taken by men, and not by bears, wolves, and ravenous hawks who resemble popish bishops and divines, because by these may be signified a devouring by hell, by those an eating of them as food for heaven."

He passed also to Wittenberg from his Patmos, making few acquainted therewith, and lodged with Amsdorf. Here he spent some few days and was merry with his friends, without the Elector's knowledge. In his retiredness, he was much troubled with costiveness, having the benefit of natural ease that way but once in four or five days. Then also was he tried by some devilish temptations, which much disquieted him. This disease he overcame by exercise, and medicines sent him from Spalatinus. Then read he also the Hebrew and Greek Bibles, and besides the books above mentioned, he wrote many letters to his friends, which are now printed.

At length not enduring further delay and innovations, he returned from his Patmos to Wittenberg, without the knowledge of the Elector, on March 6th 1522, he rendered these reasons of his return to the Elector.

"First," said he, "I am called back by the letters of the Church and People of Wittenberg – and that with much solicitation and entreaty. Secondly, at Wittenberg, Satan has made an in-road into my flock, and raised such stirs, that I cannot well repress and quiet them with my writing alone, but of necessity I must live there, be present among them, and both hear them and speak to them, go in and out before them, and do what I can for their good. Besides I fear, that some great and violent sedition will arise in Germany, and make Germany undergo grievous punishment for its contempt and ingratitude. I thought it therefore needful to do what I ought and could for them in this regard by my counsel and endeavor, to teach, admonish and exhort them, thereby to avert God's anger and judgment, or at least to stay them a while.

Furthermore, I know well, and am verily persuaded that my preaching and my proceeding to divulge the gospel of Christ is not of my own motion, but the work of God. Nor shall any kind of death or persecution shake this my confidence and make me think otherwise, and I conceive that I rightly divine that no terrors or cruelty can put out the light already shining."

And in another epistle: "I return to Wittenberg under a more sublime and strong protection, than the Elector of Saxony can give me. Nor did I ever mind to sue for defense from Your Highness. Moreover did I know that Your

Highness would and could defend me, verily I would not return. No sword can advance and maintain this cause. God alone can order and promote it, without any man's excessive care and helpful hand. Therefore in this cause, he that most strongly trusts to God's assistance, he most surely defends himself and others.

Seeing as therefore I perceive Your Highness to be weak in faith, I can by no means attribute so much to Your Highness, as to be persuaded that I can be defended and freed from danger by you. I will keep Your Highness' person, your mind and body, and estate safe from all danger and damage in this my cause, whether you believe me or not. Let Your Highness then be assured and not doubt at all, that this matter is far otherwise concluded of in heaven than at Nuremberg. For we shall find that they which think they have devoured all the gospel and quelled it in the rising, are not yet come to the Benedicite.

I have to deal with another manner and more powerful prince than our duke. He knows me, and I him conveniently well. Did your Highness believe, you should behold the wonderful works and glory of God; whereas you not yet believing, see none of these things. To God be glory and praise forever."

This and much more to this purpose he wrote, showing his full assurance and plerophory of faith most admirable. He also wrote thus to Melanchthon concerning the cause of his return: "Provide a lodging for me, for the translation of the Bible compels me to return to you; pray to God that it may stand with his good pleasure. I desire to conceal myself, as much as I can, yet will I proceed in my work resolved upon." He wrote the like to Amsdorf, that for the translation of the Bible he must return to Wittenberg, that therein he might use other men's counsel and help.

Luther – being returned from the first Lord's Day in Lent – that whole week every day preached one sermon. These are extant, and in them he showed what he liked or disliked in the alterations made in his absence. He found fault with them, who had abrogated private mass and idols, and administered the Lord's Supper in both kinds, and taken away auricular confession, differences of meats, invocation of saints, and other the like matters; not because they had done impiously, but because they proceeded not herein orderly.

He affirmed that he condemned the papistical mass, the worshiping of images, the rules of auricular confession, prayer to saints, the popish fasting; but he did condemn them only by the Word of God preached, and not by a violent abrogation of them.

How much he prevailed by those sermons, he tells in these words: "I gave offense to Carolostadt, because I blamed his proceedings, though I condemned not his doctrine. Only this disliked me: that dealing about ceremonies and outward matters, he labored less in that which is Christian doctrine indeed, namely: faith and charity. For by his unadvised course of teaching, he brought the people to this pass, that he thought himself a Christian by these petty matters, by communicating in both kinds, by not using confession, and by breaking down images," etc.

And this was the beginning of dissension between Luther and Carolostadt.

In this 22nd year,[25] the New Testament came forth, as it was translated into the German tongue in his Patmos, and afterward revised somewhat by Melanchthon. Some popish princes and bishops prohibited their people to read it. He wrote also a letter to the Bohemians concerning matters of great moment [*importance*], and exhorted them to constancy in the truth, which they had received, and that they would not fall back to Antichrist for a vain hope of peace. He also dissuaded them from making themselves guilty of the innocent blood of John Hus and Jerome of Prague. And whereas some objected their many different sects; he showed that there were many more among the papists, and prescribed the Bohemians a course, how they might cure this disease.

---

[25] In 1522, Luther translated the New Testament and printed it.

Here he inveighed earnestly against such bishops, as did condemn and persecute the doctrine of the gospel: and being often provoked did neither defend their own doctrine, nor refute Luther's. He showed them that by their tyranny they should not prevail, because he was neither moved by the pope's anathema or curse, nor Caesar's proscription, and that he would endeavor so much the more to propagate the gospel, and set to it with the more courage, by how much the more violently they withstood it; and that the gospel would not be extinguished, though they should kill him; and that God would plague them most conspicuously and grievously, if they proceeded in their furious course.

In this book, he so angered the then bishops, abbots, monks, and the whole dregs of them, that they resolved that seeing they could not burn Luther himself, they would burn all his books.

About this time also, Luther confuted Nicolas Stork, Thomas Muncer, and other fanatical ringleaders, and prophets broaching new doctrines, who pretended angelic revelations, and conferences with God, and denied the baptism of infants; and thereby sowed the seed of Anabaptism. These false prophets came from the Cygnean city to Wittenberg, in Luther's absence, and molested Carolostadt and Melanchthon.

Now also Luther answered Henry VIII, King of England, who, as other adversaries also, set out a book against Luther, and had given him by Pope Leo the title of *Defender of the Faith of the Church*. Only Luther answered him somewhat sharply: which course some of Luther's friends disliked. Of the same, thus Erasmus wrote: "If Luther – first commending the godly care of the king – had afterward with solid arguments refuted his opinions, and laid no disgrace on the king's person, I suppose he would have done that which would much have advanced his cause." Again: "What set Luther on, to say in his book against the king? Let Your Highness come to me, and I will teach you. Truly the king's book was written in a good Latin style, and not unlearnedly."

Luther thus excuses this his fact [*act*]: "If any man be offended at my sharpness towards the king, I thus answer him: In that book I have to do with senseless monsters, who contemn my best and most modest writings, and my humble submission, and are more hardened by my calmness. Besides, I abstained from bitter speeches and lies, with which the king's book is full fraught; nor is it any great matter, if I give no more respect to an earthly king, and speak sharply, seeing as he was not afraid to blaspheme the King of Heaven with his speech, and to speak profanely in his virulent lies. God the righteous judge divide the matter between us."

This book he dedicated to Sebastian Earl of Schlick, whose singular piety and zeal he commends, and says that he will make this writing the beginning of his flying to the Bohemians. For both the king and others had falsely accused him of flying thither and did triumph and brag, saying: "We have won the day, the heretic is fled to the heretics."

In the year 1523, at the Assembly at Nuremberg, the Emperor being absent, the decree made at Worms was disannulled. And when the pope's legate complained thereof, and said, that Luther was not punished according to Caesar's decree; the princes answered that most men in Germany were so instructed by Luther's sermons and books; that if that decree had been executed, it would have given occasion of great sedition; and that this construction would have been made thereof: namely, that the truth of the gospel was thereby oppressed and extinguished, and manifest errors and evils stood for, which might not be tolerated or winked at any longer; and that now this assembly was gathered, that a free council might shortly be kept in Germany at Mainz, or Argentorate, or Metz, or Cologne; and that in the meantime, Luther and others should set forth no books; the preachers should preach nothing but the gospel, plainly and modestly, according to the interpretations commonly received by the church: that such preachers as transgressed should be mildly punished, by fit men appointed by the bishops, lest anyone should suspect that this was done to hinder the free preaching of the gospel: that the printers should imprint, or divulge nothing, but what was allowed and approved by learned and judicious men; that the priests who had married wives, should be amerced [*fined*] according to the award of the pope's laws. There were here also exhibited to the legate a hundred grievances of the German nation: of which we will speak elsewhere.

This decree was diversely interpreted by several parties. Luther by his letters to the princes declared how he conceived the meaning of it: "And I – that they commanding that the gospel should be taught according to the received judgment of the church – intended not according to the course of Thomas or Scotus, but of Hilary, Ambrose, Augustine and the like." Again, that the bishops should choose fit men, who should be present at sermons, and mildly admonish such as offended, if need were. This Luther showed to be well decreed, but could never be effected, because they wanted [*lacked*] learned men. Concerning that which they decreed about books, he rejected it not: so that the decree did not extend to the sacred books of the Scripture: the publishing whereof was in no wise to be prohibited.

Lastly, concerning the amercing [*fining*] of priests who either married, or left their order, the decree was too harsh, and if the gospel was purely to be preached, ought to be mitigated. The emperor was somewhat offended with the course and was tempted by his legate to take it away, but all in vain. For this business was far otherwise concluded of in heaven than at Nuremberg, as Luther wrote. For the princes and cities of the empire strove, who first should admit the reformed doctrine. This was done in Denmark, Prussia, Livonia, Silesia, and elsewhere.

In this year, Luther set forth the book concerning the dignity and office of the civil magistrate. Frederick the Elector was much delighted with this book. He wrote also to the Waldenses, commonly called the Picards, concerning the adoring of the sacrament. In this book, he first mentions the opinion of Berengarius concerning the Lord's Supper, before he began the contention with the Helvetians.

He now also set forth the five books of Moses in the German tongue, 3,000 years since the death of Moses. He published also a book to the Senate of Prague about ordaining of ministers, and another about avoiding the doctrine of men. He wrote this year also to the Livonians, and showed his great joy at their entertaining the evangelical doctrine, which many tyrants in Germany sought obstinately to oppress, and forewarned them that they must expect cruel persecutions of the same kind: to the undergoing whereof, he gravely and piously exhorted them, encouraging them to be resolute and to persevere valiantly in the truth of the gospel, which they had received.

He further did instruct them briefly and plainly concerning justifying faith and the true nature of good works.

He this year also set forth a form of the mass and communion; herein he retained all the usual rites, which were not plainly repugnant to the Word of God, as the preface of the Psalms, the kyrie, the collect, the epistle, the sequence, the gospel, the creed, the sermon, the prayers, the preface, the *sanctus*, the Lord's prayer, the words of the Lord's supper, the elevation, the *agnus Dei*, the thanksgiving. But the canon of the mass, which transformed the Lord's supper into a sacrifice for the quick and the dead, he wholly omitted.

This was the first change of the rites, though Carolostadius had abandoned. And when two monks of the Augustinian profession were the first day of July burnt by the Inquisitor, and first shed their blood for the reformed doctrine of the faith, Luther renowned their constancy with a hymn or Psalm, and praised them as the first martyrs of his time. Of this story also Erasmus writes.[26]

Then also, Luther sent a consolatory letter to the Augustinians, which is extant amidst his works. He wrote also to the [Miltebergians], who were then in danger for

---

[26] Epist. B21, B7 & B[24] E4

the gospel's sake. Their first instructor was John Draco Carolstadius. Luther also comforted three noble Misnian virgins, which were turned out of the Freiburg Court of Henry Duke of Saxony.

Other nuns left their cloisters elsewhere, whereupon Luther wrote thus to Spalatinus: "There came to me those nine converted nuns, who left Nimptschen Monastery. Miserable is their case, but they were conducted by honest citizens of Torgan, namely by Leonard Coppe, and his uncle's son, and Wilsus Tomischech, that there is no cause of suspicion. I much pity them, but especially many other their like, who every where in great number perish by their cursed and incestuous chastity. That sex is most weak of itself, and by God's and natures appointment, is to be a mate for man, and being by papistical cruelty shut up from men is brought into perdition.

Among them was Katharina von Bora, who afterward was Luther's wife. He writes to the same, Spalatinus elsewhere of other nuns, thus: "There departed sixteen nuns out of the monastery of Widerstatten under the Earl of Mansfield, of which eleven came to the Quaestor of Alstadt. Of them Albertus received five. It is now debated among them, whether they ought to be entertained or rejected. Nor yet is here an end of our news. This year is most fruitful of novelty, and as I perceive still will be."

Luther also often was earnest with the Elector of Saxony, suing to him by Spalatinus that he would demolish the Wittenbergian Beethaven, that is the college of cursed souls. And gave this reason, Because almost all the priests there not onely live wickedly, but also are contemners of God and men with obstinate hearts, and every night play the whoremasters, and in the morning say mass with an impudent and brazen forehead. For this he called Amsdorf to witness, and said that all of them except three were wanton persons, and not to be maintained; yea, that it was the duty of the magistrates to prohibit their whoredom, and compel them to marry. For though no man can be compelled and forced to the truth: yet public wickedness is to be taken away. At the least, the masses might be forborne, which were maintained at the princes' charge, and were wickedly performed, and to no good end.

John the Prince of Anhalt – by Doctor Jerome and a Franciscan – warned Luther to acquit himself of holding a new article, with which Ferdinand of Nuremberg did charge him, namely: that he held that Christ was the seed of Abraham. At the first, Luther conceived that they jested with him: but when he found that they spoke it sadly; he was forced to give credit to their speech, that he was indeed so accused.

Pope Adrian then opposed the gospel, and by his bull, as they call it, very much blamed Frederick the Elector of

Saxony for the neglect of his duty in not punishing or banishing Luther. And then warned and entreated the prince, that now at length he would do it: and if he would not, he should try how keen the pope's and Emperor's swords were. The same request, Henry VIII King of England and Louis King of Hungary and Bohemia made. To all these, the Elector returned no other answer than that Luther was first to be heard in the council, before he was to be condemned. The pope's legate also accused Luther at the Nuremberg assembly as being most like to Mahomet: "For as the Turks by polygamy, so Luther taking away the vows of chastity does loose the reins to all licentiousness, and overthrow the state of the church, and therefore he might be condemned before he was heard; besides, as now he did show his cruelty against the ecclesiastical state, he would afterward do the like against the political."

In this year, Christian, King of Denmark, and his wife, sister of Charles V, were expelled from their kingdom for his too violent government. And being in banishment at the court of his uncle Frederick, Elector of Saxony, heard Luther preach.

In the 24th year, Clement VII – made pope in Adrian's stead – sent Lorenzo Campeggio the Cardinal, [his legate], to Nuremberg. He wrote at large to Frederick the Elector, and highly praised the pope's goodwill, and did undertake that a council should be called. Then also, Caesar and most of the princes of the empire pressed for the decree of Worms. This thing when Luther had notice of, he bewailed the state of Germany, and complained of the blindness of men.

That year, Erasmus of Rotterdam – persuaded by the King of England and Thomas Wolsey Cardinal – wrote against Luther. He put forth (against his will, as he wrote to a friend of the author) the treatise concerning free will. What was Luther's judgment about the book of Erasmus concerning free will he wrote to Spalatinus shows: "I have seen the book of Erasmus concerning free will: and yet I have scarce read eight leaves thereof. It grieves me to answer so unlearned a book of a man so learned." That book was answered by Luther in the year 1526, with which delay the minds of learned men were held in suspense, what would be the issue of the controversy.

This year was remarkable for the unhappy sacramentary controversy: the beginning and proceeding whereof is related in the life of Carolostadt, Zwingli, and Oecolampadius, and I list not here to renew our grief by opening the sore again.

About this time came forth the fanatical writing of Thomas Muncer of Stolberg, and the preacher of Alstadt: in which he disgorged his venomous fury against the Lutherans. The book which he wrote against Luther, was dedicated to Christ Prince of Princes. He railed on Luther, because he wanted [*lacked*] an enthusiastic spirit, and had nothing in his writing but a carnal spirit. The same Muncer wrote to Melanchthon a letter plainly showing his fanatical spirit.

Luther now put forth David's Psalter in the German tongue, and a book against the seditious, and an epistle to Frederick and John Princes of Saxony against the enemies of images, and enthusiasts, who boasted of illumination and conference with God. He also set forth a book about the exaltation of Benno, a bishop once of Misnia, whose bones were on the sixteenth day of May dug up at Misnia, exalted, and placed in a marble tomb: which act some took to be religious, other jested and laughed thereat.

This year in October, Luther laid aside his monkhood, and declared his judgment concerning the synod to be called for determination of the ceremonies, saying thus:

"I think it not very safe to call together a council of our men for the settling of uniformity of ceremonies, for it will set a bad example, though it be attempted with a good zeal, as appears by all councils from the beginning. So that in the apostolic synod they did more treat concerning matter of action and traditions than of faith. In the synods after this they never disputed about faith; but always about opinions and questions, that the name of councils is more suspected and hated by me than the name of free will.

If one church will not of its own accord imitate another in external matters, what need is there to compel them by the decrees of councils, which presently are changed into laws and snares to entangle men's souls. Rather let one church freely follow the good example of another, or let each church enjoy her own ways, so that the unity of the Spirit be kept entire in faith by the word of God, though there be diversity and outward ceremonies, and elements of the world."

About this time the priests of Wittenberg – keeping their popish rites – were at length evicted, and in the end of the year abrogating private mass, began a reformation in the Cathedral Church. Luther had long pressed them to this, and had written thus to Spalatinus in this year. By God's help I will abrogate private mass, or venture upon another design.

The year 1525 is famous by the rising of the boors [*peasants*], when this broil was a-hatching, and the rustic fury did not yet break forth into taking up arms, Luther did dissuade all men from sedition, as being a crime of very high nature. He also handled the articles of the boors, and showed how most of them were contrary to the Word of God. He wrote also to the princes and nobility, and put them in mind of their duty: and by another treatise exhorted all men, to join for the subversion of the thievish incendiaries, as for the quenching of a common fire. This book was censured by some as too sharp, but was at large defended by Luther.

In the beginning of this year, Luther answered Carolostadt's books, entitling his book *Against the Celestial Prophets*. At Wittenberg then the chieftains of the Anabaptists were called *prophets*, because they boasted of secret revelations, and prophetical spirits; the principal men were Muncer, Ciconius, Cellarius, and his friend Carolostadt.

Luther in the first part of his book speaks of images, private mass and Carolostadt, and affirms that images were forbidden in the Old Testament not in the New, and that Carolostadt was not expelled by his means, and that the name of *mass* was given by the apostles to the sacrament of the altar.

The subject of the second book was the eucharist, where he first dealt against Carolostadt's exposition of the word τοῦτό {*This*}, and then answered the arguments of Carolostadt, and said that the words (which is given for you) have this sense: *The body which you eat in the bread, ere long, when it is not eaten shall be given for you.* And as it is not written, *Take the body and eat it*; so neither is it written: *Take the bread and eat it.* And that Christ's speech "*The flesh profiteth nothing*" is to be taken as spoken not of the flesh of Christ, but of the sense of the flesh, which is death, Romans 8: that the breaking the bread is the distribution of the body: and that the blood of Christ which is poured out for us, now sitteth at the right hand of God; but that the efficacy of that effusion of his blood is forever. And finally, that it is unknown how the bread becometh and is the body of Christ, and that we must stick to the very words of Christ. Against this, Zwinglius and Oecolampadius wrote, as is said in its due place.

Now also Luther renewed the ordination of ministers of the gospel in the church, of whom George Rorarius was the first: and now first the mass was celebrated at Wittenberg in their mother tongue. And now was set forth a book of German songs composed by Luther and others the last year: and a book of the abomination of the mass, in which he galled the popish sore backsliders, and made many of them kick against him.

He wrote also a letter to them of Strasbourg, where he heard that Carolostadt abode, and dissuaded them from devouring his poison. On the contrary, Strasbourg sent George Caselius the Hebrew professor, and entreated Luther that he would not break the unity of the church for the controversy of the eucharist, that he would acknowledge Zwinglius and Oecolampadius – learned men and of good fame – for brethren, that he would write of the Lord's Supper, and show what he taught was consonant to the truth.

Luther returned this answer by Caselius, namely: that nothing was more to be desired than peace; but to be tied to a continual silence was not safe that answer could not be made without condemning them, and that the word *condemn* was censured as opprobrious; that he was censured of those most modest men as a cannibal, and a worshiper of God turned bread and eatable; that he liked not the advice of the divines of Strasbourg, concerning silence about the question of the bodily presence, and preaching faith and other parts of the word; that either he himself or they were ministers of Satan; and that therefore in this case there was counsel to be taken, and no mean between both to be followed; that the reasons brought to make the speech tropical were of no force; and that it must be proved, that the verb *est* not in other places of Scripture, but here is in effect *significat* that where Paul says, {*the rock was Christ*}, he speaks not of the corporal, but the spiritual drink: for he adds that they drank of the spiritual rock; and that there was a manifest mistake in that *This lamb is the Lord's Passover*, for this phrase is nowhere extant in the Scripture: and therefore he besought the brethren for Christ's sake that they would avoid this error.

Luther – being forty-two years old – all of a sudden and unexpectedly married Katherina Von Bora, a noble virgin, late a nun, and this was the occasion. Luther had a purpose that this Katherine should have been married to M.

Glanus, the pastor of Orlamund. Of this she having intimation, acquainted Amsdorf, Luther's inward friend, therewith, and by him entreated Luther to alter his determination, and to signify to him that she would enter into the honorable estate of matrimony with any other rather than with Glanus.

When Luther heard this, and what Jerome Schurfius had said – namely: that if that monk should marry her, the whole world and the devil himself would laugh thereat, and so the monk should undo all that formerly he had done – Here Luther – [in order] to grieve the world of papists and the devil, and gratify her father persuading him thereunto – resolved to marry her. And on the 13th day of June, inviting to supper Pomeranus, and Apelles the lawyer, and Luke the limner, was betrothed to her, and not long after married her.

This Luther's enemies much disliked, so did his friends also: not because they thought the marriage unlawful, but because they wished it had been done at some other time. For thus writes Camerarius: "It fell out that when these turbulent and dangerous broils were not yet pacified, Martin Luther married, not long after the death of Frederick, the chief of the seven electors of the empire. Philip Melanchthon – much grieved at Luther's marriage, not that he condemned it as unlawful, but because hereby an occasion was given to Luther's enemies and ill-willers, who were many, rich, and of great power, to speak against him bitterly, and with open mouth to reproach him – when especially the very time did help forward and set them on, who were minded so to do. And of what power the convenience of time is in every action, all know full well. But when he perceived that Luther himself was somewhat troubled with the same thoughts, he not only moderated his passion, but did cheer up Luther, and endeavored to ease his grief and sorrow with pleasant conference, and thereby brought him to his wonted cheerfulness again."

Luther's adversaries not only observed the time of the marriage, but proclaimed the marriage to be incestuous, in which a monk married a nun. Hereupon the King of England, in his answer to Luther, styles this marriage incestuous, and there saith, among other opprobriums put upon Luther, that he could not have committed a sin of higher nature.

Conradus Collinus, prior of Cologne, and Jerome Emser, the best divine among the papists, wrote virulently and disgracefully of this marriage. Yea, some there were, (whom Erasmus gave credit unto) who laid a sin to Luther's charge, from which the time of his child's birth did acquit him.

Against these disgraces Luther thus animated himself, saying: "If my marriage is a work of God, what wonder is there, if the flesh be offended at it? It is offended even at the flesh which God our Creator took, and gave to be a ransom, and food for the salvation of the world. If the world was not offended with me, I should be offended with the world, and should fear that it was not of God, which I have done. Now seeing as the world is vexed and troubled at it, I am confirmed in my course and comforted in God. So do you."

The cause of his marriage, he there also relates, saying: "We resigned the revenue of the monastery to the prince. I who abode in the monastery so long as it pleased God, now like a private housekeeper. I have not married to prolong my life, but (seeing as my dissolution nearer approaching, and people with their princes to rage against me) that I might leave my own doctrine for the weak's sake confirmed by my own example, for my doctrine may perchance be kicked against and trodden on after my death."

This year the Anabaptists spread themselves over Helvetia and other parts of Germany, and began to broach their fancies at Antwerp. Hereupon Luther by an epistle warned them of Antwerp to take heed of the erroneous spirit, which had hindered him very much, and recited the impostures of false spirits in popery, and the by-paths of the seducing spirits of the present times. There he set down the erroneous articles of a tumultuous spirit at Antwerp and opened the inconstancy, lying, boldness, and ambitious desire of honor lurking in that spirit, and entreats them to forbear the question concerning God's hidden will, and to attend to, and learn the necessary precepts set before us by our God. The articles were these:

1. That every man has the Spirit.
2. That the Spirit was nothing else but our reason and understanding.
3. That every man believes.
4. That there were no *inferi* or place of torment for men's souls, but that the body only was condemned.
5. That every soul should be saved.
6. That by the law of nature we are taught to do good to our neighbor, as we would he should do to us: and that this will in us was faith.
7. That we sin not against the law by desiring anything if our will consent not to our desire and lust.
8. That he which has not the Spirit, has not sin, because he lacks reason, which they called the Holy Ghost.

Now also Luther wrote to the King of England by the persuasion of Christian the banished King of Denmark. This epistle was submissive, and is extant in his epistles. He wrote also humbly to George Duke of Saxony, that he would be pleased to afford him his favorable respect. But the king returned him a harsh answer, and objected to him his levity and inconstancy, and defended Cardinal Wolsey against Luther's writing to him, that hence it appeared how he hated Luther. When Luther saw the king's answer printed, he was very much grieved at what he had done, and that he had so much yielded to his friends, as to write in so humble a strain. The like befell him upon his writing to Cajetan, George Duke of Saxony, and Erasmus of Rotterdam, who by Luther's lenity were incensed rather than pacified. He resolved never afterward to run into the like error. Cochlaeus and Eckius wonderfully also insulted over Luther's submissiveness. Wherefore Luther now printed a book against (as he called it) the ill-languaged and contumelious book of the King of England.

In the year 1526, Luther refused Erasmus's book, entitled *De Servo Arbitrio*. The delaying of his answer proceeded from the cause certified to Amsdorf in these words: "I will not answer Erasmus till I have done with Carolostadt, who makes great troubles and stirs in Upper Germany." Erasmus – provoked thereby – put forth his *Hyperaspistes*, of which book Luther thus writes: "Erasmus that viper, being roused up, will write against me again; what eloquence will that most vain hunter after glory exercise to cast down Luther?"

About the same time, Duke George and the bishops attempted many ways to wrong Luther, as appears by his letter to Myconius: saying: "The wicked papists conspire, and, as Melanchthon writes to me from Iena, threaten war against me. Wherefore see you, that the people admonished hereof, manfully contend by faithful and continual prayer to the Lord, that they may be overcome and withheld by the Spirit, and constrained to keep outward peace. Verily, I understand by the writings and speeches of many, that there is very great need of earnest prayer: for Satan's plots are a-working. Wherefore I entreat you, that you would persuade the people to this most necessary and prevalent work, because they are endangered and exposed to Satan's sword and fury encompassing them."

He further says that the sectaries were divided into six sects. "Six heads in one year are sprung up among the Sacramentarians. It is a strange spirit, which so much differs from itself. One sect followed Carolostadt that is fallen, a second is that of Zwinglius which is falling, the third is with Oecolampadius which will fall, the fourth also which is Carolostadt is fallen, he thus disposes of the words: *That which is given for you, is my body*. The fifth is now arising in Silesia, set forth by Valentine Crantwald and Caspar Schwenkfeld, who thus invert the words: *My body which is given for you, is this*, that is: spiritual meat. These grievously vex and molest us with their writings, for they are most obstreperous and full of words. I wish they had my disease of the stone, they seem so strong to undergo it. The sixth is that of Peter Florus at Cologne, which Melanchthon will deal with: I never saw ought but one letter about it. O how he reprobates Luther! "I know," says he, "that Luther is forsaken of the Lord. All those spirits differing each from other contend with subtle arguments, all of them boast of revelations obtained by prayer and tears, and agree only in this: that all of them fight with each other for us. This Christ effects for us."

Luther wrote a consolatory letter to John Hess of Breslau, a teacher of the gospel, notwithstanding the scandal raised by the heretics, and their fighting against the articles of our faith; and in special manner he animated him against Schwenfeld and Crantwald, saying,

"You speak the truth, friend Hess. Hitherto the combat was about points not grounded in the Scriptures, such as the pope and purgatory, and the like. Now you come to more serious matters and to the battle already won concerning points in the Scripture. Here we shall see the dragon fighting, or rather, we shall combat with him, Michael being our captain in these heavenly fights. When the dragon shall pull down the third part of the stars with his tail to the earth, then the cause will call for our strength in Christ. Here you shall see what manner of warrior, and how strong a champion Satan is, whom yet you have not sufficiently tried or experienced. Schwenkfeld and Crantwald, which I much lament, are reserved for these mischiefs. *But the foundation of God stands firm, having this seal: "The Lord knows who are his."* Let this be our comfort, and in this let us be confident to prevail over the gates of hell."

Besides other studies of Luther, he now expounded Ecclesiastes, which was not easy and plain (as he said) for an interpreter's labor. "There are," said he, "many Hebraisms and obstacles in that tongue, not yet well made known. Yet by the grace of God, I break through them." This year he wrote a form of the mass in the German tongue, in which he permitted some ceremonies to be used or not used at men's pleasure. Among other statements, he says, "Yet we retain those garments, altars, and wax candles used at the Mass, till they grow old or that it seem good to change them. If it please any man to do otherwise, I permit him to do as he likes best. But in the true mass among Christians unmixed with papists, it is fit that the altar should not remain, but that the minister should turn himself to the people, as Christ doubtless did at the first celebration of the Lord's Supper. But let this also await its due time."

He also wrote four consolatory Psalms to Mary, Queen of Hungary, upon the miserable death of her husband, King Louis, who drowned. He then also published other treatises, which are mentioned in his works.

In the 27th year, the Anabaptists broached their new doctrine about the non-baptizing of infants and were themselves rebaptized. They also taught the community of goods. Both Luther and Zwinglius wrote against them, and the magistrates punished them in various places. Luther also wrote upon the question of whether soldiers lived in a kind of life tending to happiness, in which discourse he learnedly and godly addressed many things concerning war and its discipline. He also dealt against the *Sacramentarians*, as he called them, and in his book asserted that Christ's words "*This is my body*," yet [*still*] stand firm.

Regarding the book, Luther wrote to Spalatinus, "I doubt not that I have thoroughly moved the Sacramentarians, for though my book is full of words and not so learned, yet I am persuaded that I have touched them to the quick. Bucer has written most virulent letters against me unto our Jonas; already they make a Satan of Luther. What do you suppose they will do when they are galled with that book? But Christ lives and reigns. Amen."

He also comforted the people of Halle for the death of George Winckler, their pastor, who was slain by conspiracy. He also answered John Hessus on the question of whether a Christian man may flee in times of pestilence, and on another question: whether, after the truth of the gospel is made known, a man may, for fear of tyrants, forbear to administer the Lord's Supper in both kinds, which Luther denied against the Prischanists.

About the beginning of the year 1527, Luther fell suddenly sick of a congealing of blood about his heart, which almost killed him. But the drinking of the water of Carduus Benedictus, whose virtue then was not so commonly known, he was presently helped.

But he wrestled with a far worse agony afterward on the Sabbath after the visitation of the blessed virgin. This is recorded by John Bugenhagius and Justus Jonas, who saw his affliction. Here he endured not only a corporal malady, but also a spiritual temptation, which Luther called a buffeting of Satan. It seemed to him that swelling surges of the sea in a tempest did sound aloud at his left ear, and against the left side of his head, yet not within, but without his head, and that so violently, that die he must, except they presently grew calm.

Afterward, when it seemed to come within his head, he fell down as one dead and was so cold in each part of his body, that he had remaining neither heat, nor blood, nor sense, nor voice. But when his face was sprinkled with cold water by Jonas (for so Luther had bidden) he came again to himself and began to pray most earnestly, and to make a confession of his faith, and to say that he was unworthy of martyrdom, which by his proceedings he might seem to run upon.

His will and testament concerning his wife with child and his young son, this he made: "Lord God I thank thee that thou wouldst have me live a poor and indigent person upon earth. I have neither house, nor lands, nor possessions, nor money to leave. Thou hast given me wife and children, them I give back unto thee. Nourish, teach, keep them (O thou the father of orphans and judge of the widow) as thou hast done to me; so do unto them."

But by using daily prayers and continual fomentations, after that he had sweat thoroughly, the grief by degrees decreased, so that in the evening of that day, he rose up and supped with his friends, and confessed that his spiritual temptation was far sorer than his corporal sickness. Hereupon the day following he said to Justus Jonas: "I will take special notice of the day last past: in which as in a school, I was put to the trial of my progress, and sat in a most hot sweating house. The Lord brings to the grave's mouth and fetches back again." He often makes mention of this temptation in his letters to his friends, and confirmed the faith by receiving absolution from a minister, and the use of the sacrament.

This year also, he put forth the story of Leonard Keisar his friend, who was burnt for the gospel's sake, at the command of William Duke of Bavaria. Of this man's martyrdom, thus Luther writes: "I have received the relation concerning Leonard Keisar's death, as also all his manuscripts from his uncle's son, which shall shortly be published, God-willing. Pray for me, who have been much buffeted by the angel of Satan; that Christ should not forsake me. O wretch that I am! And so much inferior to Leonard: I am a preacher only in words, in regard of him, so powerful a preacher by his suffering. Who can make me fit, that not by his spirit double on me; but by one half of it, I may overcome Satan, and put a period to this life. Blessed be God, who among so many monsters has shown us unworthy sinners this one glorious spectacle of his grace, that he may not seem wholly to have forsaken us.

Then also by the advice of Luther and the command of John the Elector, was ordained a visitation of the churches in Saxony. The chief care of this business was committed to John a Plaunitz a noble knight, to Jerome Schurfius a lawyer, Asmus Hanbicius, and Melanchthon. Many matters were hereby discovered, which needed speedy redress; many faults were found, which must necessarily be amended. Nor can I easily say how great was the benefit of this visitation. For faults of many years' continuance were reformed, the churches fallen back were in many places confirmed, and their safety for time to come was well provided for.

This visitation ended in 1528, in which year Luther put forth the institution of visitors, and the large confession concerning the Lord's Supper, which were added for their direction. There it is that Luther thus writes to Amsdorf: "We are visitors, that is bishops, and we find poverty and scarcity everywhere. The Lord send forth workmen into his harvest. Amen." And in another place to Spalatinus: "Our visitation goes on; of what miseries are we eyewitnesses? And how often do we remember you, when we find the like or greater miseries in that harsh-natured people of Vogtland. Let us beseech God to be present with us, and that he would promote the work of his poor bishops: who is our best and most faithful bishop against all the arts and forces of Satan. Amen." And again: "In our visitation in the territories of Wittenberg, we find as yet all pastors agreeing with their people, but the people not so forward for the Word and sacraments."

The first part of the book – called *The Great Confession of the Faith* concerning the Lord's Supper – deals with Zwinglius, the second part with Oecolampadius, and blameth both of them, To this, Oecolampadius and Zwinglius replied at large, and dedicated their books to the Prince of Saxony and Landgrave of Hessen. Bucer also in the German tongue answered Luther in a dialogue where he makes Sebaldus and Arbogastus speakers. These are the last books which these men wrote against Luther.

This year also, Carolostadius wrote a letter to George Pontanus, Chancellor of the Duke of Saxony; in which he laid down the groundwork of his tenets concerning the Lord's Supper. This was answered by Luther's epistle to the same Pontanus. Luther therein admonishes that care must be taken that no blemish be laid upon the elector, by whose connivance Carolostadius does there divulge his own dreams and heresies. Luther also wrote to Carolostadius, and confuted his arguments, and in the end of his letter grants, that Christ alone does give his body, but denies that thence it follows that the minister does not give it by the Lord's command.

In the beginning of the year 1529, Luther put forth his greater and lesser catechisms for the good of the lower sort of people, and admonished the pastors and ministers that they would seriously attend to their offices, and teach carefully in the villages. That they would preach still the same things about the same points and often press them upon the people. Here also Luther put forth a book against the Turk in the German tongue: this he did partly because it was then reported that the Turk was coming upon Hungary and Germany, which appeared true by his besieging of Vienna; partly because some pastors endeavored to persuade the people that war was not to be waged against the Turk. Yea, some proceeded to that height of folly, that they desired that the Turk would come and lay his yoke upon them. And when at that time there was held an assembly at Spire, where first arose the name of Protestants, and Luther's assistants, whose help he used in translating the prophets, were separated, he himself being sickly, that he might be in some employment in

Melanchthon's absence, translated the book of Wisdom which was afterward revised by Melanchthon and printed.

In October of this year, Philip Landgrave of Hessen, with a pious intent, called together the prime doctors of the Saxon and Helvetic churches – among whom Luther being sent for returned this answer: that little good was to be hoped for by that conference, except the adverse part came thither to yield. And that, [he] himself could not yield, because he was assured that he was in the truth. In this meeting, the chief heads of divinity were handled and concluded of. No one point was with choler contended about, nor did they depart alienated or divided in their affections by any controversy, as elsewhere is shown.

In the last year a fame was spread of a league made by some popish princes against the Duke of Saxony and Landgrave of Hessen: Of this, thus Luther writes to Wenceslaus Link: "That ungodly league of wicked princes, though they deny it, what stirs has it caused. But I do interpret the slight and poor excuse of Duke George as a confession of the fact. But let them deny, excuse, dissemble it; I know that that league was not a chimera or a thing of no being: a monster cannot be but monstrous and conspicuous enough. And the world knows well that they with most pertinacious minds, deeds, edicts, designs, have hitherto publicly attempted, and still do attempt the like. For they desire that the gospel was abolished; this none can deny. But why write I thus to you, who knows this to be undoubtedly true? I do it only [so] that you may know that we will not trust that wicked crew, though we offer them peace. The Lord confound the counsels of that Morotatos Moore's bundle of folly, who like Moab dares attempt more than he can effect; and as ever, so still is proud above his power. Let us pray against such manslayers. Hitherto they have been forborne; if again they plot anything, first we will pray to God, then we will admonish princes of them, that they may be destroyed without pity: seeing as they are insatiable blood-suckers and cannot be at rest, unless they see Germany weltering in her blood."

This letter intercepted and brought to Duke George gave occasion of a great disaffection between the Duke and Luther, as the letters written from each of them to the other fully manifest.

For Luther printed a treatise of letters privately sent and intercepted; and on the other side, George the Duke printed a preface to the translation of the New Testament set forth by Emser. This preface was full fraught with gall. Luther thus says of it: "I have received your letter, friend Wenceslaus, by which you certify me, what Duke George has adventured to do. He required the same of me not long ago, and afterward of our Duke. When he could not prevail, he has printed the copy of it with an invective against me: such is his notorious folly, railing fury. They say that there are 8,000 books printed, which he transports into all coasts under his own seal. Thus shall poor Luther at length be kept down, and Duke George shall triumph most gloriously. To the mart he will send them. After I by some private means had got a copy thereof, I wrote an answer thereunto, which shall be divulged at once with his writing contrary to his expectation. Perhaps he will burst with rage, and die like a miserable idiot.

I could wish that the devilish Mericion had taken it in mine own hand: I am so far from fearing that Satan: though I wonder at Scheurferus, that he not delivered my letter up to them, but that he is so familiar with my bitterest enemies. I entreat you that with your congregation you would pray against that furious homicide and bloody ruffian, as a man possessed by more than one devil, and breathing out nothing but menaces and slaughter: that it would please Christ to save him, as he did Saint Paul; or confound him. For why should this unquiet and mischievous vassal of Satan be offensive to heaven and earth?"

The remembrance of the thirtieth year will never be razed out, while men live on earth, for in this year was held that solemn and numerous assembly before the emperor and the states of the empire, which was printed and made known to all the nations of Europe. Read the story elsewhere.

We return to Luther. He composed the seventeen articles, before the divines of Saxony took their journey to Augsburg. In these articles, he omitted scholastic disputes and points unnecessary for the people's instruction, and comprised the sum of wholesome and necessary doctrine for the salvation of men's souls and true piety. Other princes and cities who embraced the doctrine of Luther commanded their divines to set down in writing a brief declaration of the doctrine commonly taught in the churches of their territories.

That these seventeen articles written by Luther were especially made use of by Melanchthon in writing the confession, the very words and phrases in most of the articles retained, and the order and method of the articles much alike, and the epistle of John Elector of Saxony dated from Augusta to Luther before Caesar's coming, do witness. For John Elector of Saxony came to Augsburg contrary to the opinion and expectation of all men – yea, he came thither first of all the princes, accompanied with John Frederick his son, Francis Duke of Lunenburg his sister's son, Wolfgang Prince of Anhalt his wife's brother, and these divines, Jonas, Philip, Spalatinus, and Islebius. For when he went from Coburg he left Luther in the castle, because he was banished by the pope and emperor, and was extremely hated by the Pontificians; yet would that he should remain in that place near at hand, that more easily and speedily he might be consulted with, for any matter pertaining to religion.

Luther – in order that he might further the common good, though he was absent – wrote a book to the bishops and other divines of note in that assembly, in which he deciphered, fully, what was the state of the Roman church under the popedom, and opened their cruelty, and exhorted them, that they would not now omit the occasion of curing this sore. He further showed that the doctrine taught by himself was agreeable to that of the prophets and apostles, and that all designs undertaken against God would be frustrated.

Melanchthon – knowing the rage of the papists and Caesar's threats – was very solicitous and troubled thereat, not so much for his own, as for the issue of these matters and posterity's sake; and gave himself almost wholly up to grief, sighs, and tears. Luther – having notice hereof – did often cheer him up and comfort him by his letters.

These words are part of one of his epistles: "In private conflicts I am somewhat weak, and you strong; and on the contrary you in public conflicts are somewhat weak, I stronger – if I may call that a private conflict, which is between me and Satan, for you are ready to die, if you were called to it, but fear the disaster of the public cause. But I am resolute and secure for the public cause, because I am assured that it is just and true, that it is God's and Christ's;

and is not appalled with the guilt of sin, as I, a private servant of God, am compelled to trembling and paleness. For this cause I am like a secure spectator, and do not regard the menaces and cruelty of the papists. If we fall, Christ the Lord and ruler of the world falls with us. And suppose he fall, I had rather fall with Christ than stand with Caesar.

Nor do you alone strive to hold up God's cause; I constantly stand to you with my sighs and prayers; I wish I might also with my bodily presence. For the cause is mine; rather I say mine than all yours: and attempted by me not out of any rash humor, or desire either of glory or gain; which thing the Spirit witnesses to my conscience: and the matter itself has already plainly showed, and will more and more show it even to the end.

Wherefore I entreat you for Christ's sake not to forget God's promises and the divine comforts, where it is said: *Cast thy care upon the Lord: have thine eyes fixed on the Lord, play the man, let thine heart be comforted.* The book of the Psalms and the gospels are full of the like speeches: *Be of good comfort; I have overcome the world.* If Christ is the conqueror of the world, why should we fear it, as if it would overcome us? A man could find in his heart to fetch such a sentence upon his knees from Rome or Jerusalem." And in the same epistle: "You would determine of these businesses according to your philosophy by reason, that is, *cum ratione insanire*, run wild with human over-care; and kill yourself: nor do ye see that this matter is beyond your reach and providence; and I pray Christ to keep it, that it come not into your hand and counsel, which is a thing vehemently desired by you. For then publicly and apparently and suddenly, we shall perish.

And in another epistle:

Grace and peace in Christ,

In Christ I say, not in the world, Amen.

Concerning your apology for your silence, I will speak elsewhere. I extremely dislike your excessive cares with which you say you are consumed. That these reign so much in your heart, is not from the greatness of the cause, but the greatness of your incredulity. For there was greater cause of this in John Hus' time than in ours. Then again suppose there be great cause, the agent and chief mover in it is of great power; for it is not our cause. Why then do you continually and without ceasing macerate yourself? If the cause is faulty, let us revoke it and flee back; if it is good, why do we make God a liar? Who has made us so great promises, and bids us to be of quiet and contented minds, saying, *Cast thy care upon the Lord. The Lord is near unto all them, who being of a troubled heart call upon him.* Does God speak these things into the wind, or casts he these pearls to brutes? I am often troubled, but not perpetually.

Your philosophy and not your divinity does thus vex you; the same befalls your Joachim. As if it were possible that you should effect anything with this unprofitable care. I pray you, tell me, what can the devil do more than kill us? I beseech you that seeing as in all other matters you are a good soldier, you would wrestle with yourself as being your own greatest enemy, by providing such a store of armor for Satan against yourself. Christ once died for sin; but for justice and truth he shall not die, but live and reign. If this is true, what fear is there for the truth, if he reign? But it will be cast down by the wrath of God, let us be cast down with it; but let it not be done by ourselves. He who is become our Father, will be the father of our children.

I pray for you earnestly, and I grieve that you make my prayers – the most violent sucking-leech of cares – to be fruitless. I truly as concerning the cause (whether it proceeds from stupidity in me or from the Spirit, Christ knows) am not troubled much, yea I have a better hope, than ever I expected: God is able to raise the dead. He is powerful also to maintain his own cause now ready to fall – yea, to raise it again, were it fallen, and to advance it, if it subsists. If we are not worthy, let it be done by others. For if we are not sustained by his promises, who, I pray you, are there in the world, to whom they do belong? But more another time; so that it be not to carry water into the sea. Christ with his Spirit comfort, teach and strengthen us all. Amen.

If I perceive that the cause goes not well with you, or be endangered, I shall not contain myself, but shall come with speed unto you, that I may see the ghastly jaws of Satan's teeth, as the Scripture calls them.

From our wilderness, January 25th, 1530.

After this, the confession written by Melanchthon according to Luther's direction and advice, was exhibited in the Latin and German tongues in Caesar's palace on January 25th, at 2 o'clock in the afternoon, and was read by the Chancellor of Saxony before Charles V, Ferdinand, and all the electors and princes being assessors – and that with so shrill and loud a voice, that not only in that large hall, but also in the court beneath and in the places adjoining it was well heard.

They who subscribed to this confession were John Duke of Saxony, George Marquess of Brandenburg, Ernest and Francis brothers, Dukes of Brunswick and Lunenburg; Philip Landgrave of Hesse, Wolfgang Prince of Anhalt; and two cities of the Empire, Nuremberg and Reutlingen. After it was read, the Prince's judgment was threefold.

First, some thought fit that the decree of Worms should be pressed, and the refractory compelled to it. Secondly, others would have had the confession examined by learned and pious men, and then to be delivered to Caesar. Thirdly, some desired that the papists should exhibit a confutation of it to the Protestants, and that the whole cause should be left to Caesar's judgment.

To this last [one], most of the princes agreed. Thereupon the Pontifician divines (of whom John Faber and Eckius were chief) were enjoined to prepare their confutation. They wrote many things bitterly against the Protestants, and rather multiplied revilings than arguments. When therefore they were bid to newly-mold their writings, the publication of the Pontifician refutation was deferred seven weeks from the exhibiting of the confession.

In the meantime, Luther and Melanchthon conferred by their letters concerning many points controverted, and discussed what might with a good conscience be yielded to their adversaries – especially concerning human traditions and matters devised by men in God's worship. Luther also by many epistles gravely written, and by exhortations full of spirit and life (which are indeed the treasures of all wholesome and powerful comfort) confirmed the hearts of the prince elector, and of Pontanus his chancellor, and their colleagues in the prosecution of their attempts for the common safety and peace of the church and state, and posterity, and for curing the apparent wounds thereof, and preventing the distractions of the church, and the confusion of opinions.

He sent also to Albertus of Mentz the Cardinal in the time of the assembly's sitting, a printed epistle. He was a man of chief authority amongst the rest; wherefore Luther endeavored to persuade him that seeing as there was small hope to settle a concord in religion, he would obtain of the Emperor at least a grant of political peace. At the same time, Erasmus wrote a letter of the same argument to Campegius.

At length, the refutation of the Protestants' confession was newly dressed and refined, and on the third day of August, was in Caesar's palace publicly read before the States of the Empire. The Emperor professed that he would persist in his opinion, and requested the Duke of Saxony, and such as joined with him, to give an assent. But, when as they could hardly obtain a copy of the confutation, and that with these conditions, that it should not be published, nor transcribed, nor any reply made thereunto, and could not prevail to have these conditions omitted; the Archbishop of Mentz, and his brother the Marquess of Brandenburg, and Henry of Brunswick requested of the Emperor that he would give them leave to take a friendly course for the composing the controversy. When Caesar had yielded thereunto, there were of each party, seven at first, and then secondly, three chosen out of each seven, who were to take a course for settling of concord.

Here when the Saxon party seemed to yield too far to the Pontifician, Luther wrote thus to Melanchthon: "Concerning obedience to be performed to the bishops, as in jurisdiction and the common ceremonies, I pray you, have a care, look to yourself, and give no more than you have, lest you should be compelled again to a sharper and more dangerous war for the defense of the gospel. I know that you always except the gospel in those articles, but I fear lest afterward they should accuse us of breach of our covenant, and inconstancy, if we observe not what they please. For they will take our grants in the large, larger, largest sense, and hold their own strictly, more strictly, and as strictly as they can. In brief, I wholly dislike this agitation for concord in doctrine, as being a thing utterly impossible, unless the pope will abolish his popedom. Concerning the confutation, this should have been added, that it was a very cold one.

Of it thus Luther wrote to Melanchthon: "Grace and peace in Christ the Lord over his enemies. I thank God, who permitted our adversaries to devise so fond a confutation. Christ is come and reigns. Let the devils, if they will, turn monks and nuns. Nor does any shape better become them, than that in which they have hitherto set forth themselves to be adored by the world."

Then a little after this: "Did not I foretell you that you troubled yourself in vain about traditions, because that point exceeds very much the capacity of sophisters? There has ever been disputation about laws amongst the wisest men, and truly it requires an apostolic ability to judge purely and surely thereof, for there is no author extant, except Paul alone, who has written fully and perfectly of this matter. Because it is the death of all human reason to judge the law: the spirit in this case being the only judge. What then can sophisters here perform, whose reason is blinded? Well, we have done our part, and well satisfied them. Now is the time of working together with the Lord, whom I beseech to direct and preserve us. Amen."

In that loving course for composing the differences by the arbitrators, when the point of invocation of saints was handled, and Eckius produced Jacob's speech, *Let my name be called upon those children*, Melanchthon first answered, and then Brentius said, that there was nothing extant in all the Scripture of the invocation of saints. Hereupon Coclaeus, that he might step in as patron to the cause, did thus excuse the matter: that in the Old Testament the saints of God were not prayed unto because they were then in Limbo, and not in heaven.

Here John Duke of Saxony concluded and said to Eckius: "Behold, O Eckius, the speech by you brought out of the Old Testament notoriously defended. The confession of our party, which Caesar, Ferdinand his brother, the princes of Bavaria, and some bishops attentively listened unto, and the other party could not endure, was translated into Italian (for the pope, who was not very well skilled in Latin) and into the English, Spanish, French, Bohemian, and Hungarian tongues."

The issue of all came to this: that though the Protestants did desire peace of Caesar, and space further to deliberate of the matter, they could not obtain their desire. The confession itself was rejected, and all who assented to it – unless they suffered all matters to run in their old tenor – were brought into hazard of their lives and states: there were some also appointed to execute Caesar's decree.

Whereas therefore it was daily expected that the Protestants should be warred against by the Pontificians, Luther – soon after the assembly with a noble and heroic spirit – set forth a book to the Germans, whose title was *Warnung an seine lieben Deutschen*, wherein he exhorted them to embrace peace, and showed that they ought not to obey a wicked edict, and further by arms the persecution of the true doctrine of the gospel, and harmless princes and churches: and fight for idols and other abominations of the papists. Yet he did not counsel the Protestant side to take up arms, before the Pontifician faction should in the Emperor's name invade them with war.

But if they should resist, and defend themselves with force of arms when they were set upon, he excused them from being traduced and condemned as seditious persons: and showed that they must be conceived to stand only upon their own and their people's defense.

Before we leave the wilderness of Coburg, and come thence with Luther, observe firstly what books he wrote there. Besides some mentioned before, of the rest he thus writes to Melanchthon: "Though I have been troubled with weariness of the task, and headache, and have laid aside Ezekiel, yet do I in the meantime translate the small prophets: and in one week more, I hope, shall finish them, by God's help. For now only Haggai and Malachi remain undone. I busy myself herein rather for the comfort I reap by them, than that I am able to undergo the pains."

Secondly, know the fervency of his prayers in this wilderness: of which Vitus Theodorus, who accompanied him at Coburg, thus wrote to Melanchthon:

"No day passes in which Luther spends not three hours at the least, and they are the hours most fit for study, in prayer. Once it so fell out, that I heard him praying. Good God! What a spirit, what a confidence was in his very expressions? With such reverence he sues for anything, as one begging of God; and yet with such hope and assurance, as if he spoke with a loving father or friend. *I know*, says he, *that thou art a Father and our God: I know therefore assuredly, that thou wilt destroy the persecutors of thy children. If so be thou please not so to do, thy danger will be joined with ours: this business is wholly thine: we adventured not on it, but were compelled thereunto. Wherefore thou wilt defend us.*

When I heard him praying in this manner with a clear voice as I stood afar off, my mind also was inflamed with a singular kind of ardency: because I observed how passionately, how gravely, how reverently, he in his prayer spake of God, and urged God's promises out of the Psalms, as one assured that what he asked should come to pass. I doubt not therefore but that his prayers will much advance and further the desperate cause treated of at the assembly."

When in that assembly the chief and almost the sole dissension between Luther and the Protestants was about the Lord's Supper: this liked [*pleased*] the papists, but grieved the Protestants.

Bucer therefore by the consent of the Duke of Saxony and his magistrates, went from Augsburg to Coburg to see what agreement could be made between him and Luther: Nor did he receive a cross answer, but diversely the business was hindered. Thither also came Urbanus Regius for to consult with Luther.

In the year 1531, Luther mildly wrote an interpretation of Caesar's edict, not against the emperor, but against the princes and bishops who were the chief instruments of the civil broils. In this he defended diverse chief heads of Christian religion, as the eucharist in both kinds; that the Church might err; the mass and free will he disallowed, and showed that we are justified by faith, not by works. Of this point observe his remarkable profession:

"I, Martin Luther, an unworthy preacher of the gospel of our Lord Jesus Christ, thus profess and believe: that faith alone without respect to our good works does justify us before God: and that this article cannot be overthrown by the Roman Emperor, nor the Turk, nor the Tartarian, nor the Persian; nor by the pope, or all his cardinals, bishops, sacrificers, monks, nuns, kings, princes, potentates of the world, and all the devils. This article, will they nill they, will stand: hell gates cannot prevail against it. The Spirit of God does dictate this unto me, this is the true gospel.

For thus the article in the mouth of all Christian children has it: *I believe in Jesus Christ crucified and dead.* Now no man died for our sins but Jesus Christ the Son of God, the one and only Son of God. I say it again and again, Jesus, the one and only Son of God, redeemed us from our sins.

This is most surely grounded and undoubted doctrine: this the whole Scripture cries out aloud, though the devils and all the world storm and burst with anger at it. And if he alone takes away the sins of the world, we verily cannot do it with our works. And it is impossible that I can lay hold on Christ otherwise than by faith; he is never apprehended by my good works. And seeing as faith alone lays hold on our Redeemer, and not our works the concomitants of our faith, it abides undoubted truth that faith alone before our works, or without our works considered, does this, which is nothing else, but to be justified, but to be redeemed from our sins. Then good works follow our faith, as the effects and fruits thereof.

This doctrine I teach, and this the Spirit of God, and the whole Christian church delivers for truth. In this I will persist, Amen."

With these two writings, *The Admonition to the Germans* and *The Interpretation of Caesar's Edict*, Luther maddened the nest of the popish hornets: who thereupon put forth a book against him, but without any man's name to it. Luther sharply answered this book, and gravely acquitted himself of the crimes objected against him, that is: that he denied yielding obedience to Caesar; that he himself was a trumpet for rebellion and sedition; that all things written by him concerning the designs of the pope were figments and lies. But he proved them to be true by many remarkable sayings and deeds of the Pontificians, which are contained in his German writings, and other books by him set out this year.

In the year 1532, by God's goodness and the intercession of the Archbishop of Mentz, and the Elector Palatine, the emperor granted peace to the Protestant churches, upon some certain conditions, propounded to the Duke of Saxony especially, which that he should most willingly embrace, Luther by his letter seriously persuaded the then present elector, and his son Frederick, who soon after succeeded his father. For this very year the 16th day of August, that godly duke – a most constant confessor of the evangelical truth – departed this life, for the perpetuating of whose memory, Luther made two funeral sermons, and Melanchthon a funeral oration at his burial, which expressed the idea or character of a good prince.

In the year 1533, Luther comforted the citizens of Oschatz by his letter, who had been turned out for the confession of the gospel. In his letter he says: "The devil is the host, and the world is his inn, so that wherever you come, you shall be sure to find this ugly host." He answered also the Elector of Saxony to this question: *How far it is lawful to take up arms in our own defense?* Especially, now there was a great controversy between Luther and George Duke of Saxony, who of old hated most vehemently Luther and his doctrine. Therefore, that the Protestant party might not be enlarged by his people's embracing it, he bound them all by oath not to receive Luther's doctrine. He also provided that the citizens of Leipzig, who, coming to confession after the Papists' manner, and then received the sacrament, should have a ticket given them, which afterward they should redeliver to the senate. About seventy were found without tickets. For these consulted with Luther what they should do? Luther answered that they should do nothing contrary to their consciences, as men who firmly believed that they should receive the sacrament in both kinds; and that they should undergo any extremity. In the epistle are these words: "Seeing as now Duke George dareth undertake to dive into the secrets of men's consciences he is worthy to be deceived, because he will be the devil's apostle."

Hereupon Duke George wrote to the Elector of Saxony his cousin-german, and accused Luther both of giving him base language, and also of stirring up the people under his command to rebellion. The elector wrote this to Luther, and told him that unless he can clear himself, he must receive condign punishment. Upon this occasion, Luther refuted this accusation, and denied that he ever counseled them to resist their prince, but that patiently they would endure their banishment; and that he was so far from infringing the authority of the magistrate, that no man did more stoutly confirm it, or more fully declare it; and that George the Duke was called the devil's angel for the subjects' sake because they should not think that the edicts were a lawful magistrate's, but the devil's.

He joined thereunto an epistle to them of Leipzig to comfort them in their banishment, and to counsel them cheerfully to undergo their present calamity, and to give God thanks for giving them courage and constancy. He told them that this rejoicing of their adversaries was neither sound nor lasting; and that it would perish sooner than any man thought; and that all attempts of the enemies of the gospel were hitherto frustrated, and by God's singular favor fallen to the ground.

He wrote also a brief apology in which he cleared himself of these crimes objected against him, namely: that he was a liar, a breaker of his promise, an apostate. Here, denying the former, he yielded himself to be an apostate or revolter, but a blessed and holy one, who had not kept his promise made to the devil, and that he was no other revolter than a Mameluke who turned Christian, or a magician, who, renouncing his covenant made with the devil, betakes himself to Christ.

To these passages, he added diverse things concerning monkery. And again in a new treatise, he opposed private mass, and their consecration of priests. In this treatise, he related his disputation with the devil, which the papists and Jesuits diversely play upon. The truth of that matter, he in this book unfolds, as being the best expositor of his own meaning. He sent also a letter to the Senate and people of Frankfurt, in which he exhorted them to take heed of Zwingli's doctrine, and instructed them about the confession.

In the year 1534, the Elector of Saxony joined in pacification with King Ferdinand. This highly grieved Petrus Paulus Vergerius, so that in the name of Pope Clement, he expostulated the matter with Ferdinand. This year Luther spent in preaching, writing treatises, and commenting. And this year the German Bible translated by him and brought into one body was first printed, as the old privilege dated at Bibliopolis under the elector's hands shows.

In the year 1535, this Bible was published. Then the fancies of the Anabaptists began to appear in Westphalia, and made a very great combustion. This year Petrus Paulus Vergerius was sent back by the pope into Germany. He spoke to the Duke of Saxony about the holding a council at Mantua. He also met with Luther, and dealt with him about matters of religion. Then Luther wrote many sermons and epistles, and a book in a popular way about prayer, and a preface to Urbanus Rhegius' book against the Monasterians, New Valentinians, and Donatists.

And when the pope had appointed the council at Mantua, Luther wrote certain asseverations [*assertions*] and theses against the Constantian (as he called it, the Obstantian) council. He sent also a consolatory writing to the Christians of Mittweida, expelled for the gospel's sake, and a letter to the Archbishop of Mentz – the last he called it, yet he wrote many after it. This year, Luther began publicly to preach on Genesis, which task he ended (as himself was wont to ominate) with his life, six years after.

In the year 1536, the form of the concord between Luther and Bucer, and other doctors in the churches of upper Germany, was written by Melanchthon at

Wittenberg, and published in the end of May. This elsewhere we spoke of, and told who subscribed thereunto.

This year Philip Duke of Pomerania at Torgau married Mary daughter of John Elector of Saxony, and of Margaret of Anhalt. Luther was at the marriage, and prayed for God's blessing upon the newly married couple. When all the rites were performed, Duke Philip reached out his hand to Luther: at this Luther stood a while silent, and still held his hand: and with a loud voice said, "The Lord God be with you, and keep your posterity from failing." Now, when as Barnim the uncle of Philip had no male children, Philip's wife for four years was barren, so that all the male stock of the Duke of Pomerania was likely to be ere long extinct. At length, by God's blessing, according to the prayer of Luther, he had seven sons by this wife, and wonderfully enlarged that noble family.

In February the year following, the Duke Elector of Saxony, with the confederate princes and cities, and their divines, held an assembly at Schmalkalden for matters of religion, that the princes might deliberate about calling the council to Mantua, and the divines confer about matters of doctrine. Hither therefore, Luther and Melanchthon were called. Luther wrote articles concerning the chief controverted heads of Christian doctrine. These the other divines did approve, and these were to be exhibited in the council of Mantua (if ever it were held) and put up in the name of the Saxon and near thereunto adjoining churches. Commonly they are called *the Smalcald Articles*. These were joined to the Augsburg Confession, and the Apology, and Luther's catechisms.

At this meeting, Luther fell sick of a grievous disease, so that there was no hope of his life. He was pained of the stone, and obstruction in the bladder eleven days. Here he – though most of his friends disliked and reasoned against it – would be carried thence; the event proved his resolution good. George Sturk the physician – being sent for from Erfurt – went along with him. Luther, as he was carried along, made his will, in which he bequeathed his detestation of popery to his friends and the pastors: as before in the house of Spalatinus in the year 1530, where he made this verse:

> *Pestis eram vivus, moriens ero mors tua Papa.*
> "I living, stopped Rome's breath,
> and dead, will be Rome's death."

But the night after his departure, thence he began to be somewhat better. At Tambach, the passages of his urine opened, so that he voided it in great abundance, and called that village the place of his happiness. This recovery of Luther was cause of great joy to many godly men, even to all who loved Luther, especially to Melanchthon, who signified the same to Luther in these words by his letter:

"I heartily thank the God of all mercy and our Lord Jesus Christ our high priest interceding for us, and compassionating our infirmities, for your recovery from your dangerous disease.

I rejoice at my heart both for your and the church's sake, that you enjoy your health again, and the rather because herein we behold the apparent love and mercy of God to his church.

Your letter expressing your recovery put cheerfulness into the countenances of the princes and all good men: they all acknowledge that the light of the gospel has been in these days made known to the world by your ministry, and know that they are beholden to you for it: and foresee what a loss it would be to the church if they should lose you. Therefore, with joint votes they pray that long you may live among us, and thank God, who has restored you from death to life. I hope God accepted this their joy and thanks. And I pray God for Christ's sake to make you perfectly sound and healthful. [...]

Here we have not yet ended our deliberation about giving Caesar's messenger an answer to his harsh dispute against our former answer. So that neither yet is any answer given to the pope.

The Duke of Wittenberg commends your noble courage, who durst in such a disease travel, and fly from this cave. He minds to follow your example, for having been eight days sick he resolves to be gone tomorrow.

[May] Christ grant that I may shortly see you in good health. I was much grieved for you, and that the more, because being absent, I could not perform any friendly office to you. I was perplexed at some physical errors, by which your disease was augmented: so that no man can express how extremity of grief wrought upon me. Nor am I yet freed from all grief. If your malady was only a difficulty of urine from some stopping,

I hope all danger is past. But if it be from the bigness of any stone, I trust that the danger will be much the less, and that you have a prudent and faithful physician, whom I pray God to direct and assist.

From Schmalkalden, 1537."

Here the pope adjourned the meeting of the Synod from the first of November to the first of May the year following, and designated the place for it to be Vicenza, a large and renowned city of the Venetians, and sent thither some of the cardinals to begin the council. He pretended a serious consultation for purging the Augean stable, and now commended the same business to some choice men, but omitted the propounding of the oath to them, and would that no man should know the intent of this reformation. Yet was it not long hidden, and as soon as it was taken notice of in Germany, Luther in the vulgar tongue, and John Sturmius in Latin, wrote to the reformers an answer.

Luther's book by a picture in the frontispiece showed its argument. For the pope was pictured sitting on a high throne with some cardinals standing round, who with fox tails on the end of long poles, as with brushes cleansed all parts above and beneath. At length all that reformation came to nothing, by whose policy and tricks it is well enough known. Luther now divulged one of the chief articles of the papists' belief (namely, concerning Constantine's donation) with annotations confuting it, for the Pontificians' sake.

He published also some epistles of John Hus, which were sent to the Bohemians in the prison at Constance in the year 1516, and wrote a preface to the [spirituality], who would be present at the council. He sent also to the pope, cardinals and prelates, the legend concerning John Chrysostom with a preface and annotations. He sent also an epistle written in a way of friendly compliance to them of the evangelical league, concerning the concord of the Helvetians, and therein showed his consent, and what was his judgment concerning the supper of the Lord.

Here, as if the church had not contentions enough already, the new sect of the antinomians start up. Their chief ringleader was John Agricola of Eisleben, who formerly had been familiarly acquainted with Luther. They held that repentance was not to be taught from the decalogue, and they reasoned against them, who taught that the gospel was not to be taught to any, but to such as were humbled by the law. And they themselves taught that whatsoever a man's life was, though impure, yet he was justified, so that he believed the gospel.

Thus Luther was put to a new pains, and at large confuted them, and showed that the law was not given that we might be justified by it, but [rather] to show us our sins, and to terrify our consciences. Therefore, the law was first to be taught, and the gospel afterward, which shows the Mediator. John Agricola – being better instructed by Luther – acknowledged his error and revoked it under his own hand in public.

About this time, in the year 1538, near Whitsuntide, Melanchthon being rector of the university for the summer half-year, one Simon Lemnius put forth a book of epigrams, by which some thought the fame of diverse men and women was blemished. Luther hereupon showed himself to be, as ever, a detester of such notorious libels, and wrote an epistle to the Church of Wittenberg in which he inveighed against the author of the libel, and showed how he disliked the course of this base poet. But the author escaped, and afterward by most impudent lying set forth such filthy and impure writings, that all good people judged that he was not to be pardoned for his former folly: and that whatever evil befell him, it was far less than his wickedness and madness deserved.

This year also were put forth the three ecumenical creeds with Luther's annotations and exposition.

In the year 1539, deliberations were agitated with much care and difficulty concerning the obtaining of peace from the Emperor: because many feared an attempt unjustly to oppress the state. Luther, therefore, together with his colleagues of Wittenberg, composed and put forth a treatise concerning a defense lawful, approved, and not contrary to God's will. And because now the name of the council and church were in every man's mouth, Luther put forth a book in their mother tongue concerning both of them. In the preface whereof, he says that the pope by calling a council does play with the church of Christ, as they do with a dog who offers him a crust of bread on the point of a knife, and when the dog takes it, knocks him on the nose with the handle thereof, to make such as see it laugh.

Luther in that book declared the authority of the Scriptures, and then treated of the councils Apostolic, Nicene, Constantinopolitan, Ephesine, and Carthaginian. He shows what a council is, which is to be called true, what are the signs and works thereof: and that Christian schools are perpetual councils; and therefore they are with great care to be maintained, as much advancing the good of the ecclesiastical, political, and economic hierarchy on earth.

About the conclusion of the Smalcald Assembly, April 24, George, Duke of Saxony, died childless, and declared Henry, his brother, with his sons Maurice and Augustus his heirs upon condition that they should not alter the religion: which if they should attempt, he bequeaths his whole territories to King Ferdinand, to have and hold the same, until the condition was observed. But while the ambassadors treated with Henry about the same, making glorious propositions to him, and promising him mountains of gold, he resolutely denied to do it: George died before the ambassadors could return; so that George, otherwise than he intended, held Henry for his heir. Hereupon in Misnia was presently made such an alteration, that whereas in Easter holidays the papistical priests preached; at Whitsuntide, Luther and his scholars had free possession of the pulpits. So Luther here began Reformation; others after him added perfection thereunto.

In the year 1540, it was decreed that the divines should meet at Haguenau on the Rhine, and peaceably confer about the doctrine of controverted points. Melanchthon – journeying thither – fell into a grievous disease at Vinaria, so that there he stayed and made his will, and prepared himself for death. Hither Luther and Cruciger, at the Elector's instance, took their journey both by night and day. Here Luther – finding Melanchthon pitifully consumed with the disease, weeping and sighing – cried:

"How excellent and useful an instrument of the church do we find miserably sick and almost dead." And when he had saluted him, he fell down on his knees, and heartily prayed for him; and then performed what friendly offices he could by comforting, admonishing, and sometimes chiding the sick man.

Of this, Melanchthon thus wrote to Camerarius: "I cannot by words express what pains I have undergone, into which sometimes I have a relapse. I perceived also that Doctor Luther was much afflicted in mind for me; but he concealed his sorrow, because he would not increase mine. And endeavored to cheer me up with his noble courage, sometimes comforting, sometimes reproving me somewhat sharply. Had he not come to me, I would have died."

This year, Robert Barnes, a learned divine, was burned at London the last of June, for witnessing to God's truth. He was familiarly known to Luther upon his coming to Wittenberg in the embassy about the divorce made by King Henry. Luther caused the confession of this his friend, and the faithful martyr of Christ, to be printed with his preface; and besides, admonished the pastors by another peculiar treatise to inveigh against usurers and usury.

In the beginning of the year 1541, Luther wrote a consolatory letter to Frederick Myconius lamentably spent with a consumption, and affirmed that he could have no joy to live if Myconius died, and thereupon wished that he himself might first lay down the tabernacle of his weak body, and said that he was verily persuaded that his prayers should be granted for Myconius' life, as indeed it came to pass: for Myconius outlived Luther six years, and would say that Luther obtained this for him by his prayers.

After Easter, Bernard, the infant son of John of Anhalt, was baptized at Dessau. Here Luther preached two sermons to the courtiers, the brother of the Prince of Anhalt, and the Bishop of Brandenburg: which were printed. He wrote also an answer to a railing book of one whom he calls Hans Wurst, wherein he defended himself and his doctrine, against the papists and their popish errors. He put forth also an exhortation to prayer against the Turk, and answered the prince's questions concerning transubstantiation, free will, justification by faith, and other points.

About this time, the bishopric of Neuburg, by Sala, was void; there Nicholas Amsdorf – a divine born of a noble family – was installed by Luther at the command of the Elector of Saxony, the patron of that diocese, and Julius Pflug, whom the Canons of the College chose, was refused. Luther placed him in the bishopric on January 20th, 1542. This thing, as many conceived, gave occasion to other stirrings, and very much offended the emperor, who much affected [Pfugius] for diverse respects. Of this see more in Amsdorf's life. After this, Luther wrote a book in the

German tongue, and called it *The Pattern of the Inauguration of a True Christian Bishop.*

He published at that time the Alcoran, which by Richard, a Dominican, was translated into the vulgar tongue. He added to it a faithful admonition concerning the abandoning of the Turk's doctrine, and affirmed that not the Turk, but the pope was Antichrist. And upon a difference arising between the Elector of Saxony and Maurice concerning the territories and town of Wurzen, so that war was likely to ensue, Luther with weighty reasons in his letters dissuaded both the princes from their designs. He further also opened his judgment about a position some years ago by him propounded, namely: that to war against the Turk was nothing else but to fight against God, who uses him as his whip to scourge us. Now also he wrote a consolatory letter concerning abortive births and bringing forth dead children.

The years 1543 and 1544 produced many great troubles and stirrings. For now the sacramentary contention began afresh, to Melanchthon's great grief, whom some attempted to set at jars with Luther. Some there were also who sought to cool Luther's heat, and spoke little more favorably of the Rhenan churches than of the Turks. Wherefore, when Christopher Froschover, the printer of Zurich, sent Luther a copy of his Tigurine Bible then printed, Luther admonished him by his letter that he should not publish anything that came to him from the ministers of Zurich, and that he had nothing to do with them, nor would receive or read their books; that the churches of God could not join in communion with them, who already were running into the way of perdition, and would bring others into hell and damnation; and that he would oppose them with his prayers and books while he lived.

And now Luther first wrote against the Jews, and refuted their lies and their blasphemous conceit about *Shemhamphorash*: the name of God expounded. He also wrote his judgment, and a short answer to Caspar Schwenckfeld's book and letter, whom he bade not to mention him in his writings, and sent him away with this answer: "The Lord reprove Satan who is in you, confusion befall the spirit which called you, and the course which you run, and all the Sacramentarians and Eutychians, who partake with you, and all your blasphemies. You do as they of whom it was written: *they ran and I sent them not; they spake and I commanded them not.*"

He wrote also his mind to others concerning the ceremonies and excommunication: he desired that there should be few ceremonies, and they tending to edification, and that excommunication should be brought into the church as a profitable discipline, but could scarce hope to see it. He admonished the young students at Wittenberg to avoid fornication, with which some then were taxed – yea, he threatened that he would hold no society with men of that ill condition: and tarried some time at Merseburg with the Prince of Anhalt. But afterwards, he was called to his ordinary task by the university, sending for him an honorable embassy. About this time, he wrote an excellent commentary upon the last words of David, wherein he soundly and plainly declared the article of the Trinity, the distinction of the persons, and Christ's deity and humanity.

In the year 1544, he finished the first part of his commentaries on Genesis, in which he often blamed the Sacramentarians, and foretold that after his death many would oppose Luther's doctrine. Then in September he published the brief and last confession concerning the Eucharist: wherein he expressly explained what in the Lord's Supper is received by the worthy receivers, what by the unworthy; what by faith, what without faith: and censured Zwingli, Oecolampadius, and others at Zurich, who set forth an apology of their doctrine the year following.

This very year, the 17th of November, he finished his explication of Genesis, which was his last public reading in the university, which he concluded with these words: "Thus end I my explication on Genesis; God grant that others may more rightly and truly expound it than I have done. I cannot proceed farther therein: my strength fails me: pray for me, that it would please God to grant me a quiet and comfortable departure out of this life."

This year in Italy was spread a most impudent lie about Luther's death. The sum of it translated out of the Italian is this:

"A stupendous and rare miracle which God ever to be praised showed about the filthy death of Martin Luther, a man damned both in body and soul, so that it conduced to the glory of Jesus Christ, and the amendment and comfort of godly men.

When Martin Luther was sick, he desired the Lord's body to be communicated to him, which he receiving, died presently. When he saw that he must die, he requested that his body might be set upon the altar, and be adored with divine worship. But God – to put an end to his horrible errors by a great miracle – warned the people to abstain from the impiety which Luther invented. For when his body was laid in his grave, suddenly so great a stir and terror arose, as if the foundations of the earth were shaken together. Whereupon all at the funeral, trembling, were astonished, and after a while lifting up their eyes, beheld the sacred host appearing in the air. Wherefore with great devotion of heart, they placed the most sacred host in the holy altar. Whereupon the fearful noise ceased.

But in the night following, a loud noise and rattling much shriller than the former was heard about the sepulcher of Luther, which awoke all the city, terrified them, and almost killed them with astonishment. In the morning when they opened the sepulcher, they found neither his body, nor his bones, nor any of the clothes. But there came a sulfurous stink out thereof, which almost overcame the bystanders. By this miracle, many were so amazed that they amended their lives for the honor of the Christian faith, and the glory of Jesus Christ."

When this lie came printed into Germany, Luther did subscribe with his own hand, words to this purpose: "I Martin Luther do profess and witness under mine own hand, that I on the 21st day of March received this figment full of anger and fury concerning my death, and that I read it with a joyful mind, and cheerful countenance.

And but that I detest the blasphemy, which ascribeth an impudent lie to the divine Majesty, for the other passages, I cannot but with great joy of heart laugh at Satan's, the pope's, and their accomplices' hatred against me. [May] God turn their hearts from their diabolical maliciousness. But if God decrees not to hear my prayers for their sin unto death, then [may] God grant that they may fill up the measure of their sins, and solace themselves to the full with their libels, full fraught with such like lies."

This year Luther set forth a book entitled *Against the Papacy Ordained by the Devil*. In this, he treats of the council appointed by the pope, and often adjourned or translated from place to place, and of other plots of the popes. There he speaks of the Campanian, who coming out of Germany into Italy, turned his bare breech towards Germany, using words to the disgrace of the nation.

Luther published diverse other treatises as the explication of Christ's speech, *Search the Scriptures*, and *The Blindness and Ingratitude of the World* in handling Christ's complaint of Jerusalem. By Luther's advice especially, Georgius Anhaltenus undertook the government of the Church of Merseburg. Of this is spoken in the life of Duke George.

In the year 1546, Luther accompanied with Melanchthon visited his own country, and returned again in safety. Not long after, the Council of Trent being begun, and having sat once or twice, Luther was called again by the Earls of Mansfield to his own country, [in order] to compose a dissension among them concerning their bounds and heritages. Luther was not wont to deal in matters of this nature, having been versed in sacred studies all his lifetime. But because he was born at Eisleben, a town in the territories of Mansfield, he was willing to do his country service in this kind. Wherefore, making his last sermon at Wittenberg on the 17th day of January, he took his journey on the 23rd day, and at Halle in Saxony lodged at Justus Jonas' house, where he stayed three days because of the roughness of the waters, and preached the 26th of January upon Paul's conversion.

On the 28th day, being Thursday at Halle, he passed over the river with Justus Jonas and his own three sons, and being in danger of drowning said to Dr. Jonas; "Think you not, that it would rejoice the devil very much, if I and you and my three sons should be drowned?" When he came to the Earls of Mansfield, he was entertained by a hundred horsemen or more of the court, and was brought into Eisleben very honorably, but very sick, and almost past recovery: which thing he said did often befall him when he had any great business to undertake. But using some means for cure of his infirmity, he sat at supper with the company, and so continued to do from the 29th of January to the 17th of February, and treated of the differences for whose determination he came thither.

In this time, he preached sometimes, and twice received the Lord's supper, and publicly received two students into the sacred order of the ministry, and at his lodging used much godly conference at table with his friends, and every day devoutly prayed. The day before his death, though he was somewhat weak, yet he dined and supped with the company, and at supper spoke of diverse matters, and among other passages asked whether in heaven we should know one another, when the rest desired to hear his judgment thereof.

He said: "What befell Adam? He never saw Eve, but was at rest in a deep sleep, when God formed her; yet when he awaked and saw her, he asked not: *what is she*, or *whence came she*, but said that she was flesh of his flesh and bone of his bone. Now, how did he know that? He – being full of the Holy Ghost and endowed with the knowledge of God – thus spoke. After the same manner, we also shall be in the other life renewed by Christ, and shall know our parents, our wives, and children, and all about us, much more perfectly than Adam knew Eve at her bringing to him."

After supper, when he went aside to pray, as was his custom, the pain in his breast began to increase: whereupon, by the advice of some there present, he took a little unicorn's horn in wine, and after that slept quietly an hour or two on a pallet near the fire. When he awoke, he betook himself to his chamber, went to bed, and bidding his friends good night, admonished them who were present, to pray God for the propagation of the gospel, because the Council of Trent and the pope would attempt wonderful devices against it. Having thus said, after a little silence, he fell asleep, but was awakened by the violence of his disease after midnight. Then complained he again of the narrowness of his breast, and perceiving that his life was at an end, he thus implored God's mercy and said:

"O heavenly Father, my gracious God, and Father of our Lord Jesus Christ, thou God of all consolation, I give thee hearty thanks that thou hast revealed to me thy Son Jesus Christ; whom I believe, whom I profess, whom I love, whom I glorify, whom the pope of Rome and the rout of the wicked persecute and dishonor. I beseech thee, Lord Jesus Christ, to receive my soul. O my gracious heavenly Father, though I be taken out of this life, though I must now lay down this frail body, yet I certainly know that I shall live with thee eternally, and that I cannot be taken out of thy hands." He added moreover: "God so loved the world, that he gave his only begotten Son, that every one who believeth in him should not perish, but have life everlasting." And that in the 68th Psalm, "Our God is the God of salvation: and our Lord is the Lord, who can deliver from death." And here, taking a medicine, and drinking it, he further said: "Lord, I render up my spirit into thy hands and come to thee." And again, "Lord, into thy hands I commend my spirit, thou, O God of truth, hast redeemed me."

Here, as one falling asleep and without any bodily pain that could be discerned, he departed this life. And when Doctor Jonas and Caelius said, "O reverend father, do you die in the constant confession of that doctrine of Christ, which you have hitherto preached?" he answered so as he might be heard: "Yea," which was the last word he spoke. Thus he in his native country, not having seen it many years before, died much lamented by many. This fell on

February 18th, on the day in the calendar ascribed to Concord, about three o'clock in the morning, in the great climacteric year of his age. Soon after, his body – put into a coffin of lead – was carried in funeral manner to the Temple of Eisleben, where Justus Jonas preached.

Then the Earls of Mansfield desired that his body should be interred within their territories, but the Elector of Saxony required that it should be brought back to Wittenberg. In the return thereof, which way so ever it went, it was honorably attended, and with much grief accompanied out of each prince's dominion, and at length upon the 22nd of February in the afternoon, was brought to Wittenberg, and was carried into the temple near adjoining to the castle, with such a troop of princes, earls, nobles, students, and other people, that the like was seldom or never seen in that town. When the funeral rites were performed, Pomeranus preached to an assembly of many thousands. And after that, Melanchthon, with many tears and sighs, made a funeral oration. When this was done, the coffin with his body was put by the hands of diverse learned men into the tomb near to the pulpit in which he had made many learned sermons before diverse princes, electors, and the congregation of many faithful Christians. On a brazen plate, his picture, lively deciphered, was there set up with verses by it to this effect:

"This sepulcher great Luther's corpse contain;
This might suffice; yet, read these following strains:

Here, in this urn does Martin Luther rest,
And sweetly sleep in hope to rise most blessed.
By whose rare pains, firm faith, and Christ's free grace,
Which formerly thick fogs of error base,
And dusky clouds of works desert bid quite,
Were well reduced to their ancient light.
For, when blind Superstition ruled all,
And did fair Truth, long time, suppress, and thrall,
He, by God's Word and Spirit's inspiration,
The gospel's light re-spread, for every nation.
And, well-instructed by Paul's sacred voice,
(scorning Rome's cheats) to teach pure truth, made choice.
And, as John Baptist, in the wilderness,
Did God's lamb, who heals sin preach and express:
So (O Sweet Christ) did Luther clear thy book,
When all the world was caught with error's hook.
And, what the difference was betwixt the law
(Whose tables Moses brake, though God he saw,
Upon Mount Sinai) and the gospel sweet,
Which heals sin-conscious hearts, which God's wrath meet.
This difference, lost, to the world He did restore,
That, so, Christ's gifts of grace might shine the more;
He stoutly did oppose Rome's cheats and charms,

And Papal rule, which wrought God's saints great harms.
Exhorting all, Rome's idols for to fly,
He many souls won to true piety.
And, maugre all Rome's threats and snares most sly,
Finished, in Faith, his course, most valiantly.
Dying in peace, his soul with Christ does rest,
Crowned with immortal glory, truly blessed.
For which rare doctor let both high and low
Bless God, that they so clear Christ's truth do know.
And pray the Lord that these his gospel's rays
May to the world shine forth for dateless days.
Philip Melanchthon.

Dead is grave Luther, worthy all due praise,
Who set forth Christ, in faith, illustrious rays.
His death the church laments, with sighs sincere,
Who was her pastor, nay, her patron dear.
Our Israel's Chariots and Horsemen rare,
Is dead, with me, let all sad sables wear;
Let them their grief in groaning verses sing,
For, such sad knells, such orphans, best, may ring.
Theodore Beza.

Rome tamed the world, the pope tamed Rome, so great;
Rome ruled by power, the pope by deep deceit.
But, how more large, than theirs, was Luther's fame,

Who, with one pen, both pope and Rome did tame?
Go, fictious Greece, go tell Alcides, then,
His club is nothing to great Luther's pen.
John Major.

By Luther's labors, Leo the tenth is slain;
Not Heracles' club, but Luther's pen's his bane.
Joachim a Beust.

When Luther died, then, with him died, most sure,
A crown, and credit of religion pure.
His soul soared up to heaven, on concord's day,
Which tended Luther, thither, on his way:
Dear Christ, since discord followed with coats rent,
Give to thy spouse Elijah's ornament.

> Upon his tombstone the University of
> Wittenberg, as to her beloved
> father, engraved:

***MARTINI LVTHERI THEOLOGIAE
D. CORPVS H.L.S.E. QVI ANNO
CHRISTI M.D.XLVI. XII. CAL.
MARTII EISLEBII IN PA-
TRIAS. M.O.C.V. AN.
LXIII. M. III. D. X.***

Thus Luther ran his course, and this was the period of his travels. When first Melanchthon heard news of his death, he uttered these sacred words of the Scripture: "The chariot and horsemen of Israel is gone," and took his death most heavily. For they had lived together 28 years in the most religious manner, so that Melanchthon truly loved him for his admirable virtues, and was a faithful mate and helper to him in clearing the doctrine of the gospel. For though those times were prone to distractions, and men's wavering minds desirous of dissension, yet when as each knew others' infirmities, there never fell any jar between them, which caused any alienation of their affection, or parting of their company and fellowship.

But what and how great storms rose in Germany after the death of Luther (out alas!) each Christian knows. So that Luther said truly, and often foretold: "That whilst he lived, by God's help, there would no war be raised in Germany; but when he was dead, the age to come would see the event."

Concerning the doctrine of the gospel, he uttered this heavenly truth: "These things will be a great bane to Christian religion. First, forgetfulness of God's blessing on us in restoring to us the gospel. Secondly, security, which already commonly and everywhere reigns. Thirdly, worldly wisdom, which would bring all things into good order, and cure the public stirrings with wicked counsels."

There was in this worthy man of God a quick and prudent understanding, a magnanimous and noble spirit. He was ever constant in known truth, from the confession whereof he could never be removed with threats or promises. So that when upon a time, one papist demanded of another: "Why do you not stop the man's mouth with gold and silver?" The other answered: "See, this German beast cares not for money."

There appeared in him a singular proof of his valor and noble courage in the Augsburg Assembly, when thus he wrote out of his wilderness to Spalatinus:

"That kings and princes and people, rage against the Christ or anointed of God, I esteem it a good sign, and think it much better than if they flattered. For thereupon follows that he that dwells in heaven laughs at them. And when our Lord and King laughs, I see no cause why we should weep before their faces. He laughs not for his own sake, but for ours, that we rather trusting to him than to anything else, might laugh at their vain designs: so much need is there of faith, that the cause of faith may not be looked upon without faith.

But he that begun this work, he began it without our counsel and contrivance; and he himself will forward with it, and finish it without, and beyond all our counsels and devices – of this I make no question; I know and am assured hereof. He in whom I believe is able to do above all, which we can ask or conceive.

Though Philip Melanchthon contrive and desire that God should work according to, and within the compass of his counsels, that he might have wherein to glory. and say, *Surely thus the business should be carried; thus would I have done.* But this is not well spoken: *I Philip would have it so.* This *I* is too flat and dull; too low a style. It must be thus: *The God, who saith, I am that I am; this is his name, I am; He will have it so.' It is not yet seen who he is, but he will appear, as he is, and we shall see him. But I have done.*

Be you valiant in the Lord, and put Melanchthon in mind from me, that he set not himself in God's place; but fight against that ambition of deity, which was inbred and took root in us in paradise by the devil's suggestion: for that is an affectation not furthering the business now in hand. The desire of being like God, thrust Adam and Eve out of paradise, and it alone does trouble us, and turn us out of the course of peace. We must be mortal men, and not gods. Thus in brief, if we think otherwise, everlasting unquietness and anguish of heart will be our reward."

Luther was ready for martyrdom once or twice, and thought his adversaries would have him to it: whereupon at his going to Augsburg in the year 1518, thus he wrote to his dear friend Melanchthon: "Show yourself a man of resolution, as you already do. Teach the students God's truth. I am going (if God so please) to be sacrificed for them and you. For I had rather die, and never more enjoy (which thing alone would be most grievous to me) your most sweet society, than to recant and revoke any truth which I have preached, and give occasion to overthrow the right course of studies."

And elsewhere he thus wrote to Spalatinus: "I had rather – as I have often said – die by the hands of the Romanists alone. And would by no means that Charles and his counselors should interpose themselves in putting me to death. I know what misery befell Sigismund the Emperor after the martyring of Hus: how nothing prospered with him afterward, how he died without male issue, how his daughter's son Ladislaus also died, and so had he his name extinguished in one age of men; besides, Barbara his queen became a dishonor to the royal place she held; and other matters which you well know. But yet if it so please God, that I shall be delivered into the hands not only of the papists and spiritual governors, but of temporal magistrates also, the Lord's will be done. Amen."

And again, thus to Lambert Thorn imprisoned: "I rejoice with you most heartily, and give thanks to our Lord and Savior Jesus Christ, that he has not only graciously given me the knowledge of his Word, but made me see a plentiful and glorious increase of his grace in you. Wretched man that I am! It is reported that I first taught those things for which you suffer, and yet shall be the last, or perhaps shall not be vouchsafed at all, to be made partaker of your imprisonments and martyrdoms. Yet herein will I challenge something, and comfort myself in this, that your miseries, your bonds and imprisonments, the fires prepared for you are mine also; and so indeed they are, seeing as I profess and preach the same things with you, and suffer and rejoice together with you."

God – by Luther and his fellow workmen – opened and cleared the necessary doctrine of God's church concerning the mediator and justification of man before God, of the differences of the law and the gospel, of worship pleasing God, of invocation, and other points. He was wont often to deplore the ungodly praying to the saints departed, and said: that there were many reasons, why that invocation was execrable, and that this was one chief, namely: that by that profane custom the testimony of Christ's divinity was obscured, to whom both the writings of the prophets and apostles attribute the honor of invocation.

These are the idols which sharpen the barbarous sword of the Turk to cut off our necks. Nor will he ever be kept from shedding our blood, except in godly manner those things are reformed. For how wicked and impious those hymns are, which are sung in the pope's choirs, who knows not? *O Mary, thou Mother of Grace, defend us from our enemy, and in the hour of death receive us.* **And again:** *Saint Dorothy create a new heart within us; Saint Catharine translate us from the troublesome sea of the world to the pleasures of paradise; open paradise for us.*"

And that God's truth might be propagated to posterity, with continual and great labor and study he so plainly and perspicuously out of the original texts translated the Bible into the German tongue, that his translation may well serve instead of a commentary.

He often speaks of the labor and difficulty of this task, as in his letter to Wenceslas Linck: "We are now busied in translating the prophets, a work (God knows) of great pains and industry, to bring Hebrew writers to speak the German tongue; to leave their Hebrew idiom, and express themselves in our barbarous language. This is as if the nightingale should be compelled to imitate the cuckoo, to leave her warbling melody, and fall into a unison."

And again to Spalatinus: "In translating Job, we are put to very great pains in regard of the loftiness of the style, that this book may seem more impatient of our translation than Job himself of his friends comforting him. He may seem yet still to sit upon the dunghill. Unless perhaps the author of the book desired that it never should be translated. This is the reason why the press makes no better haste in this part of the Bible."

In this work, he used the pains and counsel of his colleagues, whom elsewhere we have named, that they might be witnesses of his faithful care in dark places. He entreated Spalatinus to send precious stones from the court, for his better knowledge of them, and took care that he might know the names and differences of certain beasts and fowls, and creeping things, and insects. He had rams, sheep, and calves killed and cut up at his house, and learned the names of their joints and the propriety of speech about them from the butchers. Oftentimes, as himself relates, he spent fourteen days together in the interpretation of one word or line with Melanchthon and Aurogallus' help.

In their consultation, this was their course: Luther was president in the work performed in the monastery, and ever had by him the old Latin translation, his new one, and the original text. To Melanchthon's care was commended the Greek Bible; to Cruciger's the Hebrew and Chaldee. Other professors were employed in the perusing of the rabbis, and every one of them still came to the work well premeditated. Every one gave his judgment concerning the place to be translated, they compared all together, and at length concluded of the expression thereof.

But Luther before his death revised the first edition, for *one day teaches another*. For this pains, we owe him perpetual thanks, for it much benefits the church, and informs such as know not the original – yea, it much pleasures the learned in the tongues for conference of translations. Yet this pains was blamed by Vicelius and Staphylus and other vassals of the pope.

Luther also published many learned expositions and comments on the Scripture, of which thus says Erasmus: "In one leaf of Luther's commentaries is more solid Divinity than in many prolix [*verbose*] treatises of the Schoolmen, and other [such] like." He also refined and much enriched the German tongue: he translated out of Latin, some things which others thought not possible to be rendered in the vulgar tongue, and yet used most significant and proper words, so that some one word might seem to set the whole matter forth most expressly.

Of the pope, Luther wrote how he made use of the mass even for the souls departed, and says that he with his mass had gone not only into all corners of the world, but even into purgatory itself. Here he uses a word in the German tongue signifying the noise of his tumbling down into hell. Also, he calls indulgence-mongers *purse-threshers* because the pope winnowed good money out of that chaff. There are full many such passages in his German writings.

Well therefore said renowned Sturnius concerning him: "Luther may be reputed very well the master of our tongue, whether you speak of the purity or copiousness of it. The counselors of princes, the judges of cities, all secretaries, all ambassadors and lawyers attribute this praise to him being a divine. The cause defended by him was just and necessary, and of itself deserved the victory; but assuredly he shot forth the darts of his arguments with the strong arms of true oratory. If he had not revived religion, if he had preached no sermons, had he written nothing else, but what he divulged of the Scriptures translated, yet for this his pains, he deserved very excellent and perpetual glory. For if the Greek and Latin, and other translations be compared with the German, they come short for clearness, pureness, propriety, and agreeing with the original. I am persuaded that as no painter could pass Apelles, so not any writer can go beyond Luther for his translation in our tongue."

He began a matter, as was conceived, beyond the reach of man; and liable to extreme danger. But there is no counsel, no power prevalent against the Lord: who most admirably defended Luther living and dead against all his adversaries. Whilst he lived, he had most potent, most subtle enemies, and in a word, all Antichrist's kingdom; nor only did the pope and his bishops, his universities and other sophisters openly set upon him with bulls and treatises published, but designed to take him away closely with poison, daggers, guns, and other means.

Concerning secret plots against him, they are well known. He thus speaks of them: "There is here a Polonian [*Polish*] Jew hired with 2,000 crowns to poison me. My friends have disclosed the plot to me by their letters. He is a doctor of physic [*medicine*], and dare attempt anything, and will go about it with incredible craft and celerity. This very hour I caused him to be apprehended; what the event will be, I cannot say. This is the news."

To Spalatinus also, he wrote that there were many actors of the plot, whom he would not have wracked if they would not voluntarily confess by whom they were suborned [*induced*], but endeavored to have them set at liberty. Yet he adds: "Though I am fully persuaded that he was the man described unto me, all marks of him did so rightly answer the description sent to me."

Again, what the papists did attempt, the words of Alexander the pope's legate do well declare. Of this, Luther thus speaks: "Spalatinus writes that Alexander was bold to say; 'Though you Germans – who pay the least sums of money to the pope – have shaken off the yoke of servitude, yet we will take a course that you shall be consumed with civil broils, and perish in your own blood."

Concerning the fables and lies cast abroad in his lifetime, what should I say? Of his country and parentage, it was bruited [*rumored*] that he was a Bohemian, and born of (as they call them) heretical parents. Then they laid aspersions upon his promotion at Wittenberg, and defamed it with sundry lies. Hear what he wrote to Spalatinus: "That ambassador, or I know not what of Ferdinand's, was with me, to see what manner of man I was, and how I carried myself. He said that it was told his master, that I went up and down armed and guarded, and did spend my time among queans, diverse tavern hunters, and was notorious among all men, with I know not what other the like honors. But I am now well inured [*accustomed*] to such lies."

How often was he reported to flee to the Bohemians? How often were scandals raised from his writings? How often was he called a *flatterer of princes*, a *trumpet of sedition*? His bold speech and vehemency was a string much harped upon.

Whence he says of himself: "Almost all men condemn me of too much eagerness. But I am of your mind, that it is God's will to have the inventions of men in this manner thus revealed. For I see matters in this our age quietly handled to be quickly forgotten, and no man to regard them."

And again: "Yet do not I deny, but that I am more vehement than is fit: which thing seeing they know so well, they should refrain from provoking me. How hard a thing it is to bridle the pen, you may well enough learn by yourself. And this is the reason why I have ever been averse from showing myself in public matters; but the more averse that I was, so much the more was I carried against my own desire, yet never – unless most grievous wrongs were done – the Word of God or myself for its sake. Whereupon it fell out that had I not been apt by nature to vehemence and embittering my style, the very indignity of the matter would have urged a dead and stony heart to write sharply: how much more myself, who am of an ardent spirit, and write not a dull style. Monsters of men carried me beyond the due temper of modesty."

For the warrant of this sharpness he used to allege the example of Christ, who called the Jews *an adulterous and perverse generation, a generation of vipers, hypocrites, children of the devil*; and Paul's example, who calls them *dogs, vain babblers, seducers, illiterate* – yea, Acts 13 most sharply inveighs against the false prophet. Moreover, Erasmus often used to say, "In regard of the height of the diseases of this last age of the world, God has sent them a sharp physician." Also Charles the Emperor said, "If the pope's priests were such as they should be, they would not need a Luther."

Further, he had diverse spiritual temptations and terrible buffets of Satan, as namely in his sickness at Coburg and at other times when his body was weak. These much afflicted him, and sometimes made him lie as one dead; but by physic applied for his cure, and reading the Scripture, and singing of Psalms, which he used to call them about him unto, he was recovered and eased of those affrights and esteemed them but as the devil's traps, from which God would deliver him.

In the dismal war of Germany, scarce could the soldiers be restrained from exercising their cruelty upon his dead corpse. For when Wittenberg yielded to the Emperor Charles and he came to see the town, the Spaniards would have dug up Luther's tomb and burnt his body. Charles V (as faithful witnesses have related) said, "Suffer him to rest till the day of resurrection and the judgment of all men."

But in the beginning of Luther's preaching, he minded not to have proceeded so far as the issue drew him to. For in the year 1520, he thus wrote: "I will offer them silence with all humility, so that others are also silent. For I will omit nothing on my part which may conduce to peace, and have ever been careful so to do. I will therefore make ready a humble letter to the pope. If matters prove calm, as I hope, it is well. If not, it is well also, for it is God's pleasure so to have it."

He often purposed also to have departed from the papists' malice. For thus he writes to Spalatinus: "Had not your letter come to my hands, I had prepared to have gone out of the way. And yet I am ready to be gone or to stay." And again, "I have not free liberty to speak or write. If I go hence, I will pour out my whole mind and offer my life to Christ."

He daily more and more discerned God's truth and could not wind himself out of some errors in the beginning presently. For about the invocation of saints thus he wrote in the year 1518: "My good Spalatinus, I never judged that the worship of saints was superstitious, nor the praying to them for matters especially pertaining to the body. For thus our neighbors, the Pighard heretics in Bohemia, conceive. For we in better manner obtain of God by his saints any good thing (for assuredly all good is God's gift) than others get by magicians and wizards of the devil, as the manner is. But this my meaning was: that it is superstitious – yea, ungodly and wicked – to beg of God and the saints things corporal only and to neglect the things which concern the soul and salvation, and are sued for according to God's will, as if we forgot or believed not his word, saying: *Seek first or chiefly the kingdom of God, and all these things shall be added to you.* Yea, everywhere Christ teaches us to slight corporal matters and our bodies as base things in regard of our souls."

Concerning the adoration in the sacrament, thus he wrote: "I say it is free for us to adore Christ and call upon him *sub sacramento*: under the sacrament. For he sins not who does not adore, nor does he sin who does adore."

Concerning the administration of the Lord's Supper in the vulgar tongue, thus he wrote: "I wish the mass might be used in the mother tongue rather than can promise to have it so, because I cannot bring it to pass, as being a matter requiring both music and the spirit. So in the meantime, I permit every man to abound in his own sense until Christ enables me to say more."

He first celebrated the mass in the mother tongue in the year 1525, as he writes to Langus and the members of Erford: "This day we attend the prince's command. The next Lord's day, we will publicly sing in the name of Christ, and mass shall be in the mother tongue for the lay people. But the daily service shall be in Latin, but we will have the lessons in the vulgar tongue. These things you shall have shortly published."

Luther caused psalms in the German tongue to be used. Concerning this, thus he wrote to Spalatinus in the year 1524: "We intend – according to the example of the prophets and ancient fathers of the church – to make psalms or spiritual songs for the common people, that the Word of God may continue among the people, if not otherwise, yet surely in psalms. We seek for poets where we may. Now, seeing as you have attained both the free use and elegance of the German tongue, I entreat you to take some pains with us in this business and try how you can turn a psalm into verse, as I have given you a pattern. I would have you not to use late invented and courtly terms, but make the verse to suit the simplest and most vulgar capacity, yet let the words be smooth and proper. Let the sense also be clear and as near as may be to the original, yet may you use this freedom as to vary the words sometimes, so that you keep the sense. I cannot perform the work so neatly as I would, and therefore desire to try how near you can come to Heman, Asaph, or Jeduthun."

He taught many things soundly and gravely about the Scripture and the authority thereof, as that our faith was to be built on the canonical books, the other books required our judgment. Of the Word, the sacraments, and ministers, he taught that we are planters and waterers and are ministers of the Word of life and sacraments of salvation, but are not givers of the increase.

Concerning our justice, he said: "Thou, Lord, art my justice; I am sin. Thou hast taken what I am, and given me that which was thine. Thou hast taken that which thou wast not and given me that which I was not."

Concerning ceremonies, he said: "I condemn no ceremonies but those which are contrary to the gospel."

Concerning Moses: "As the learned men of the world say that Homer is the father of all the poets, the fountain, yea the ocean, of all learning, wisdom, and eloquence, so our Moses is the father and fountain of all the prophets and sacred books, that is: of all heavenly wisdom and eloquence."

Concerning human learning: "I am persuaded that theology could not wholly be kept sincere without the skill of other arts. For heretofore, when knowledge of other learning was decayed or despised, theology did fall and lay neglected most miserably. Nay, I discern that the revelation of God's Word would never have become so glorious unless first the tongues and arts had been brought into use and flourished and made a way for divinity, as John Baptist did for Christ. And elsewhere, I think they err and are extremely out of the way who think the knowledge of philosophy and of nature to be of no use for theology."

Of temptations, thus he speaks: "I would have men who are tempted thus to be comforted with faith and hope: first, to avoid solitariness and still to have company and to sing psalms and talk of holy matters. Then, secondly, to be assuredly persuaded (which though it be most difficult, yet is it the most ready cure) that those thoughts are not their own but Satan's, and therefore that they should earnestly endeavor to turn their hearts to some other thoughts and leave those evil thoughts to Satan. For to insist upon them, to strive with them, or to struggle to overcome them is a provoking and strengthening them to a man's perdition without remedy."

Of men distracted and fools, this was his judgment: "I think that all fools and such as have not the use of reason are vexed or led aside by Satan, not that they are therefore condemned, but because Satan does diversely tempt men, some grievously, some easily, some a longer, some a shorter time. And whereas physicians attribute much to natural causes and mitigate those evils by natural means sometimes, this comes to pass because they know not how great the power and strength of the devils are."

Concerning the assembly at Augsburg, whose remembrance Melanchthon delighted not in, because there such as endeavored the propagation of the gospel were censured by Charles V harshly and grievously. Whereunto 5 electors, 30 ecclesiastical princes, 23 secular princes, 22 abbots, 33 earls and barons, and 39 free cities subscribed.

Of this assembly, I say, this was Luther's judgment: "Though after much expense you see nothing done at Augsburg, yet thus I think: though their cost had been double, yet the public confutation of the sophisters and envious persons would be equivalent thereunto, for they sought to disgrace our doctrine with lies as if it was the most erroneous that ever was heard." Of it also Brentius says: "The cost bestowed in all assemblies within the memory of men is not a sufficient price for the excellent treasure of the confession and apology."

Of the Lord's Supper, thus Luther writes: "I neither can nor will deny this, that if Carolostadius or any other man within these five years could have persuaded me that there was nothing in the sacrament but bread and wine, he should have done me a singular kindness. For I have labored much and been most studious about this point's discussion. I have endeavored with all possible intention of mind to clear and fully open this matter, because I well saw that hereby I could especially wound the papists. Besides, I had two others who wrote to me more soundly and acutely of this point than Carolostadius, nor did so wrest the words to the conceit of their own humor. But I saw myself fast taken and had no way left to escape. For the text of the gospel is so clear and powerful that it cannot be shaken, much less be overthrown with words and glosses suggested by addle-heads."

Of this question, he wrote a large epistle and endeavored to prove that Christ's flesh was not only eaten spiritually, but corporally. And whereas elsewhere he speaks otherwise of this matter, there are some who affirm that he opened his mind thereof a little before his death. For it is said that as he was fitting himself for his journey to Eisleben, on January 23rd, 1546, he affirmed to Melanchthon that he confessed that he had gone too far in the sacramentary controversy. And when Melanchthon persuaded him to explicate his mind by publishing some book, he answered that by this course he should derive a suspicion on all his doctrine as faulty; but Melanchthon might do as he saw cause when he was dead. The witnesses of this his speech are Melanchthon, Herbert de Langen, Daniel Burenius, cons. of Bremen, and others.

When Antonius Musa, the Pastor of Rochlitz, on a time complained that he himself could not believe what he taught others, Luther answered: "I thank God that I hear others to be affected to the papists' doctrine as I was." He was wont to say that a preacher should beware of bringing three dogs into the pulpit with him: pride, covetousness, envy.

This rule he gave concerning the government of one's self in preaching: "When," says he, "you see the people hear most diligently, conclude that they will go away more cheerfully."

He judged them in princes' courts to undergo the greatest labors who are compelled to drink so extremely that they cannot rest night or day. When a stone was brought unto him out of the Mansfeld stone pits, wherein was the image of the pope with a triple crown, "Lo," said he, "the pope must be revealed and extolled by metal mines and diggers of metals."

"Three things," said he, "make a divine: meditation, prayer, temptation. And three things were to be done by a minister: (1) he must read the Bible over and over; (2) pray earnestly; (3) always be a learner. And they were the best preachers to the people, who spoke as to babes in Christ, in the ordinary strain, popularly and most plainly. When he visited the churches in Saxony, and a countryman repeated the words of the creed in the vulgar tongue, saying, *I believe in God the Father Almighty*, he asked the countryman what was meant by *Almighty*, who answered: *I know not.* Luther said, *Neither do I nor any learned man know it. Only believe that God is your Father and that he can and will preserve you and yours.*'

He took delight to express some things in his own tongue and in rhyme, of which some were to this sense and meaning:

"Eat what is sodden well;
Drink what is pure and clear;
That thou the truth doth tell,
To all let it appear.

Speak not to all whatever thou dost know:
If thou be well, keep wisely where thou art:
Conserve with care whatever is thine own,
Mischance sure-footed comes like the nimble hart.

Be silent in due time, abstain, sustain,
Hold up thy head. Of need to none complain.
Despair not of God's help, thy state to stay:
Who sends assistance to us every day."

He was in his private converse of such behavior that his life was a pattern of virtue. As he dined or supped, oftentimes he would dictate matter to be preached, sometimes correct the faults of the press, and sometimes he would recreate himself and others with music. He was by nature (which Melanchthon would often wonder at) a moderate eater and drinker, and yet had no small or weak body. He has been seen for four days together, and being in health, to eat and drink nothing at set meal times; and often at other times for many days to be content with a little bread and fish. I will say nothing of how in the cloisters he macerated himself with watchings, fastings, labors.

Oftentimes, being invited to banquets, he went not, because he would not lose his time. "I," said he, "lose too much time by invitations to feasts here in the city. I know Satan has such a hand in it that I may not deny it, and yet it does me harm to accept the courtesy." In company, he was familiar, pleasant, courteous, yet grave, as befitted a man of his place. He was affable and studious of truth.

Melanchthon affirms that he often found him at prayer with great ardency and tears, imploring God for the whole Church. He set apart every day a certain time for reading some psalms and intermingled his own prayers and tears with them. He often used to say that he was offended with those who, either through idleness or variety of employment, said that it was enough to pray with groans only. "And for that end," said he, "forms of prayer are prescribed to us by the will of God, that reading might inflame our minds – yea, that the voice also might profess what God we call upon."

When he recreated his mind and took it off from study, he delighted to play at chess and was skillful at it. He sometimes practiced the art of turning with his servant

Wolfgang, and would say: "If the world should deny us sustenance for my pains in God's Word, we would learn to get our livings with our hands." Sometimes he did play on an instrument; sometimes shoot. He was careful also of the neatness of his garden and desired of his friends a variety of plants to furnish it, so that he had no vacant time.

Of his employments, thus he writes: "I am very full of employment: the Psalter requires a whole man, preaching to the people might well require all my pains, my course of worshiping God and prayer might wholly busy me; my pains in expounding Scripture by writing, my writing epistles, my care of other men's affairs takes up my time, my converse with my friends (which I use [*tend*] to call a feeding of my corpse) does very badly steal away a great part of my time." It was his usual course either to meditate, or to read, or to preach, or to give good counsel to his friends, so that he was never idle.

He was very liberal to the poor. On a time when a student asked some money of him, he bade his wife to give him something; and when she excused the matter in regard to their penury at that time, he took up a silver cup and gave it to the scholar and bid him sell it to the goldsmith and keep the money for his occasions. When a friend sent him 200 angels of gold from the metal mines, he bestowed them all on poor students. When John the Elector gave him a new gown, he said that he was made too much of: "For if here we receive a full recompense of our labors, we shall hope for none in another life." When the same elector offered him a vein of metals at Sneberg, he refused it, lest he should incur the temptation of the devil, who is Lord of treasure under the earth.

He took nothing of printers for his copies, as he writes, saying: "I have no plenty of money, and thus yet I deal with the printers: I receive nothing from them for recompense of my many copies, sometimes only I receive of them one copy. This I think is due to me, whereas other writers, yea, translators, for every eight leaves have an angel." Concerning money given him, thus he writes: "The hundred angels given me I received by Tanbenhem, and Schart gave me fifty, that I stand in fear that God will give me my reward here. But I protested that I would not so be satisfied by him. I will either presently repay it or spend it. For what should I do with so much money? I gave one half of it to P. Prior and made him a joyful man."

He was very lovingly affectionate towards his children and gave them liberal education. He kept in his house a schoolmaster to train them up in good arts and a godly life. When he saw Magdalena, his eldest daughter, ready to die, he read to her that in Isaiah 26:19: "Thy dead servants shall rise again, together with my dead body shall they arise. Awake and sing ye that dwell in the dust: for thy dew is as the dew of herbs, and the earth shall cast out the dead.

Come, my people, enter into thy chambers and shut thy doors about thee: hide thyself as it were for a little moment, until the indignation be over-passed. My daughter, enter thou into thy chamber with peace: I shall ere long be with thee. For God will not permit me to see the punishments hanging over the head of Germany." And upon this, he wept plentifully. But in public, when he went along with the hearse, he bridled his affection and was not seen to shed one tear. And as all men of excellent spirits have a zealous anger in due place, so Luther by nature was vehement, but yet placable. As appears in this: when Melanchthon – much moved to passion – once came unto him, and all the rest were very mute, Luther uttered this verse:

> *Vince animos irámque tuam, qui caetera vincis.*
> "Thine own heart overcome, thy fury tame,
> Who all things else hast stoutly overcame."

And then, smiling, said: "We will not further dispute of this matter," and turned his speech to other occasions.

He foresaw and foretold many things, as the combustion which rose in Germany, saying: "I am very much afraid that if the princes give ear to Duke George's ill counsel, there will arise some tumult, which will destroy all the princes and magistrates in all Germany and engage in it all the clergy." Of the death of Frederick, Elector of Saxony, thus he writes: "If God in heaven has resolved in wrath to deal with us, that neither our prayers nor counsels of amendment can hinder it, let us obtain this: that our Josiah may sleep in peace, though the world be left to go into its Babylon."

Of the covetousness of Germany and the dearth there, thus he speaks: "We fear famine, and we shall suffer it, and find no remedy for it. And when, without necessity, we are solicitous to prevent famine, like wicked and incredulous Gentiles, and neglect the Word of God and his work, he will permit shortly a dismal day to come upon us, which will bring with it whole wain-loads [*wagon loads*] of cares, which we shall neither have power nor means to escape." Diverse other things he also foretold.

He had his health competently well, but sometimes he was troubled with headache – especially in his elder years. Whereupon he was afraid of some violent apoplexy, and when he felt a swimming in his head or noise in his ears, he used to say: "Lord Jesus, smite me gently, for I am absolved from my sins according to thy word and am fed unto life eternal by thy body and blood. Thine Apostle John and our Elector were taken out of this world by this kind of death."

He endured often temptations, whereupon he said: "All here are in health except Luther, who is sound in body and without suffering at no man's hand in the world; only the Devil and all his angels vex him."

He was of an indifferent stature, of strong body, of so lion-like a quickness of his eyes that some could not endure to look directly upon him when he intently beheld them. They say that one of mild spirit, who could not endure in private to talk with Luther, was courteously used by Luther, yet was so pierced with the quickness of his eyes that, being amazed, he knew no course better than to run from him. His voice was mild and not very clear, whereupon, when on a time there was mention at table about Paul's voice, which was not very perfect and full, Luther said: "I also have a low speech and pronunciation." To whom Melanchthon answered: "But this small voice is heard very far and near."

In wedlock, he lived chastely and godly above twenty years, and when he died, left three sons and Katharina von Bora a widow, who lived after his death seven years. To her, it was a great grief that her husband died in a place far from her, so that she could not be with him and perform the last conjugal offices to him in his sickness.

In the time of the war which presently followed, she wandered up and down with her orphans, and in banishment was exposed to many difficulties and dangers. Besides the miseries of widowhood, which are full many, the ingratitude of many did much afflict her. For where she hoped for kindness in regard to her husband's worthy and noble deserts of God's church, often she was put off with great indignity.

When afterward her house at Wittenberg in time of pestilence was infected, she, for her children's safety, as became a godly mother, betook herself to Torg, where was also a university. But on the way, when the horses, affrighted, ran out and seemed to endanger the wagon, she – amazed not so much for her own, as her children's preservation – leapt out of the wagon. Poor wretch, she grievously bruised her body in the fall and, being cast into a pool of cold water, caught thereby a disease of which she lay sick three months in banishment and, pining away, at length died quietly in the year 1552.

Luther's writings were published at Wittenberg and Jena in several towns, both in Latin and the German tongue. Part of them were expositions of Scriptures, part doctrinal, part polemical. Of these, this was his own judgment:

"Above all, I beseech the godly reader, and I beseech him for our Lord Jesus Christ's sake, that he would read my writings judiciously and with much pitying of my case. And let him know that I was formerly a monk and a most furious papist when I first entered into the cause undertaken by me – yea, I was so drunk and drowned in the opinions of papism that I was most ready to kill all men, if I could, or to assist and consent to their attempts that did kill them, who even in one syllable should dissent from the pope. Such a Saul was I, as some that are yet alive. I was not so cold and calm in defending popery as was Eckius and his mates, who more truly for their bellies' sake seemed to defend popery then that they were serious in the cause – yea, they seem still to me to laugh at the pope in secret, as Epicureans. But I proceeded in the pope's defense earnestly because I set before my eyes the last day of judgment and trembled thereat, and desired from my very heart to attain salvation."

In another of his writings, he in a manner wished his books extinct, saying: "Alas, my friends should not trouble me. I have enough to do with the papists, and might almost say with Job and Jeremiah: *Would I had not been born* – yea, almost say: *I would I had not published so many books, and would not care if they were all perished*. Let other such spirited men's writings be sold in every shop, as they desire."

Luther also was much against it that any man should be called a *Lutheran* after his name. Because the doctrine was not his, neither did he die for any one. Against this humor of men also Luther said: "How should it come to pass that I – a sack of worms' meat – should be accessory to this: that the children of Christ should be called after my base and unworthy name?"

He also much opposed the title of *Lutherans* because we are all Christians and profess the doctrine of Christ: as also because the papists are guilty of this crime, by calling themselves *Pontificians*. We ought not to imitate them in evil.

Of Luther's books, thus writes Sturmius: "I remember that in an epistle of Luther's to Wolfgangus Capito, which is in Conradus Hubert's library some years ago, I read that he himself took content in none of his books but only in his Catechism and his book against free will."

For a conclusion, I will here add Melanchthon's judgment concerning the talents by God bestowed on Luther and others:. "Pomeranus," says he, "is a grammarian and explains the force of words; I intend logic and show the context of the matter and the arguments; Justus Jonas is an orator and copiously and elegantly discourses. But Luther is all these: a very miracle among men. Whatever he says, whatever he writes, it pierces men's minds and leaves behind it a wonderful sting in their hearts."

Camerarius speaks thus of Luther: "The name of Luther is so odious to some that they detest the hearing of it; on the contrary, others endure not that anything should be found fault with, which either he spoke or did. And if any man dare speak against him, they declaim against him presently as one guilty of impiety. They who thus extol the name and authority of Martin Luther, as not doubting to elevate him above the condition and measure of mortal men, should see to it that they do not wrong the good name of so excellent and admirable a man by attributing too much to him, and that they do not seem to shelter and protect their audaciousness under his excellency. And those calumniators, who not only condemn all his writings as ungodly and turbulent, now also, if they had any wit, might remember and consider what is gained by bitter envy, contumacy, froward opposition, and outrageous clamors."

Wolfgang Severus, tutor of Ferdinando of Austria, afterward Emperor, wrote a distich encomiastic upon Luther to this purpose:

> Of Japheth's race hath Luther's like ne'er been,
> And his superior, sure, will ne'er be seen.

His impress was a rose and a cross, the explication whereof is this:

> A rose and cross great Luther's heart disclose.
> The rose, his joy; the cross, Christ's yoke, he chose.

Thus have we described Luther's life and death out of his own and other learned men's writings: in perusing whereof, the reader is to be entreated (which thing Luther himself requested concerning his whole works) to judge well what he reads and to consider well whence Luther came, and at what time he wrote, namely, out of the dark mists of popery, and when the rays of the gospel began again to show themselves.

FINIS.

www.ingramcontent.com/pod-product-compliance
Lightning Source LLC
Chambersburg PA
CBHW020243010526
44107CB00002B/79